explore humanism

Mark Vernon

flash.

Hodder Education

338 Euston Road, London NW1 3BH.

Hodder Education is an Hachette UK company

First published in UK 2012 by Hodder Education

British Library Cataloguing in Publication Data: a catalogue record for this title is available from the British Library.

10 9 8 7 6 5 4 3 2 1

www.hoddereducation.co.uk

Typeset by Cenveo Publisher Services.

Printed in Great Britain by CPI Group (UK) Ltd, Croydon, CR0 4YY.

Also available in ebook

Contents

Introduction

A humanist is someone who believes that human values, experience and imagination are the best tools we have for living a good life and making sense of the world in which we live.

The first individuals in the West whom we can say were inspired by a recognizably humanist vision were the Ancient Greek philosophers – individuals like Socrates, who proposed that human beings might enquire about the nature of the world and about how they should live.

The Renaissance humanists, who are defined by their rediscovery of the philosophers of antiquity, delighted in the human capacity to create, not least in wonderful works of art. Humanists of the Enlightenment realized that human reason had a tremendous capacity to pursue questions about truth and meaning too, and further, that human beings could take responsibility for the answers they gave to both.

In this book, we'll pick up the story in the Victorian period, when individuals called themselves humanists for the first time. They organized themselves to campaign for rights and freedoms that they argued were fundamental and core to what it is to be human. Then, across the twentieth century, and into the twenty-first, the humanist tradition has inspired champions of secularism, individuals who are seeking to work out what it means to live without resorting to religious faith.

They are not the only people who call themselves humanists today. Paradoxically, there are many religious individuals who think of themselves as humanists too, because they place human individuals at the centre of their faith, and not, say, the authority of the church or of the Bible. Then, there are artists and writers who are called humanists, because they seek to explore the human condition in their work.

But across this diversity, there is a common theme: a delight in, curiosity about and commitment to being human, however that is conceived. Humanists of all persuasions can be said to keep that view of things before them.

1

the origins of modern humanism

Today, humanism comes in a variety of forms, and we begin our exploration with three philosophical traditions whose impact on humanistic thought today can hardly be underestimated.

The first is that of Karl Marx, the philosopher who noted that religion is the heart in a heartless world, as well as the opium of the people. His lasting legacy in the West is social democracy, the desire to construct an economy with the human good in view.

The second tradition we'll consider is the humanism associated with the philosophy of utilitarianism. The principle of utility is that something is good if it promotes happiness and decreases pain, and this is an important goal for many contemporary humanists.

The third is the great American philosophy of pragmatism that can be summarized as 'what works', the notion that truth is relative but that should be enough for us humans.

From the mid-nineteenth century onwards, various post-Enlightenment thinkers started to refer to their philosophy as humanist and, soon after, others started to refer to themselves as humanist or humanistic. It is in this period that, various systems of thought emerged that were first self-identified as humanism. In this chapter, we will look at what were historically the first three of these developments, Marxism, utilitarianism and pragmatism.

1 **Marxism** The first is, of course, associated with the philosophy of Karl Marx. As far back as 1844, Marx had written of an explicitly modern idea of humanism in his *Economic and Philosophical Manuscripts*.
2 **Utilitarianism** The second development is associated with the philosophy of utilitarianism, the idea that an action is right if it tends to produce happiness and wrong if it does the reverse. This approach actually reaches back into the eighteenth century, but here we will pick it up in the work of John Stuart Mill, who published his seminal text called *Utilitarianism* in 1861.
3 **Pragmatism** The third is a tradition of humanism that developed first in the US, in the shape of the pragmatism of William James. He argued that usefulness and practicability are the criteria by which to judge the merit of ideas. Pragmatism was dominant during the first quarter of the twentieth century, and it still has its champions today.

In each case we will consider the origins of the philosophy concerned and then how it manifests itself in humanism now.

Marxism

In some ways Marxism can be seen as originating in a criticism of one tendency within Enlightenment thought and humanism alike, namely a powerful valuing of the individual. The worry is that a society which gives itself over to such individualism rapidly turns into one where it is only the powerful and wealthy who can exercise their free choice. The Marxist critique therefore suggests that what is required is not a theory of ethics and the individual, but ethics and society. In other words, what is sought is a socialist theory of the human condition – socialist in the broadest sense. To be human is to be one of many, a social animal.

In fact, before Marx appeared and made this approach his own, socialist theories of various sorts had been associated with the humanist tradition. It could be said to reach back to Plato who was fond of the Ancient Greek aphorism: 'Friends hold all things in common.' His exploration of the ideal society, *The Republic*, revolves around the belief that nothing is more damaging to human beings than social division.

Thomas More's *Utopia*, one of the great products of Renaissance humanism, reflects on socialist ideals too. On his eponymous island, there is no such thing as private property or even privacy; doors are kept unlocked. Almost everyone shares in the work that must be done and this makes light of it; citizens only have to labour for six hours a day.

Of course, both Plato's *The Republic* and More's *Utopia* are also implicit critiques of such socialist ideals. Plato paints a picture of common life that is at least as disturbing as it might be appealing. More's neologism – utopia – literally means 'no place'. And it was not until the nineteenth century that Marx picked up the baton and tried to iron out the difficulties to arrive at a socialist theory that could be put into practice on a large scale. In his early work at least, he explicitly associated the word humanism with his version of socialism, namely communism.

Alienation

In the *Economic and Philosophical Manuscripts*, Marx identifies the damage that is done to human beings who live under individualistic capitalism and explores the human potential that he imagines would be liberated under a socially based, communist regime. He sees the issue as coalescing around a tension that human beings have always struggled to resolve, namely the tension between the fact that they are 'of nature', though live in often very unnatural societies.

Marx believed that human beings find their self-realization in nature: through labouring on the land they change the world and change themselves in the process. However, he also saw that the needs of human beings can only be met when they co-operate. A tension arises because this social side of human life is opposed to the former naturalism. In other words, we must learn to labour *together* if we are to thrive.

But this is a struggle, and it gives rise to ever-more complex modes of production and patterns of interaction, such as those we call capitalism. However, they are also a source of problems. For under capitalism, human beings are alienated from themselves because the satisfaction that might be gained from being productive is lost. Why? Because capitalism distances people from the fruits of their labour. They work for a capitalist boss who creams off the profits. This exploits the worker and leaves them not only without much to live on but possibly in outright poverty. The result is a sense of alienation. It is experienced not just materially but existentially as well. Our social essence has become separated from our natural existence. We are alienated from ourselves.

Religion as opiate

Incidentally, this explains the origins of religion according to Marx. Religion arises as the 'opiate of the people', in the famous phrase, a palliative against the horrors of alienation. It is the 'sigh of the oppressed creature, the heart in a heartless world, the soul of soulless conditions,' as Marx also said of theistic belief. However, although Marx was avowedly atheistic, he did not believe that simply identifying the causes of religion, or exposing its fantasies, would be enough to throw it off. Only when the realities of humankind's alienation had been practically addressed would religion disappear, for it would then be no longer necessary. Conversely, it would be ridiculous to believe that religion could simply be 'thought away' if people's material conditions were left unchanged.

Marx believed that the time when this would happen was coming. The form of that coming was communism. He thought that the pressures of living under capitalism were becoming unbearable. The moment was arriving when human beings would rise up and communism would be born, the period of history in which people's material natures would be reconciled with their social natures. It is this reconciliation that he calls a form of humanism in this passage from the *Economic and Philosophical Manuscripts*.

> ***Communism as completed naturalism is humanism, and as completed humanism is naturalism. It is the genuine solution of the antagonism between man and nature and between man and man.***

Totalitarianism

Of course, we now know that communism did arise, but not with the happy results for which Marx longed. Far from reuniting the essence of human beings with the lives they could lead, it propagated atrocious violence. The combined activities of Stalinism, Maoism and other totalitarian communist regimes amounted to the slaughter of tens of millions of human beings during the course of the twentieth century.

For humanists, it is important, therefore, to ask where Marx went wrong. Philosophers have pointed to the way Marx underestimated the capacity of capitalism to reinvent itself, and so keep human beings' revolutionary tendencies at bay. Others have pointed to economic flaws in his system.

However, another area that might be of particular interest to humanists concerns his misunderstanding of human nature. We have outlined his belief in its productive, labouring essence. What is striking about his insistence on the centrality of labour in human nature is that it appears to ignore the many other characteristics that philosophers have thought equally important, such as, say, personhood, language or indeed religion.

Marx's argument is that these are important too, but labour always takes priority: personhood, language and religion depend upon labour as their source. In other words, they all depend upon our productive capacity.

Universality

Marx also argued that human beings share a universal nature. By this universality he meant that all things being equal – notably under a communist regime – people would experience a powerful sense of solidarity with one another. His hope was that this fellow-feeling would eventually transcend all the barriers between peoples that exist under capitalism; barriers such as nationality and religion – a hope that is captured in the famous slogan that concludes the tract which Marx penned with his friend and collaborator Frederick Engels, *The Communist Manifesto*: 'Workers of the world, Unite!'

Again, though, it seems that this force of sympathy is just not substantial enough to power the emergence of global communism. Or since that would now seem to be an undesirable outcome anyway, one might wonder whether human fellow-feeling even has enough potency to overcome the excesses of capitalism that continue to flourish in the modern world. Which takes us back to the original question: is there a socialist ethic that could appeal to contemporary humanists and that can be made to work?

Socialist humanism

Modern socialism can be thought of as the political philosophy that draws on Marx's analysis of capitalism – which is powerful and lasting for all the failures of communism – while rejecting the specifics of his communist solution. In fact, what was called 'socialist humanism' was a self-conscious reaction to the horrors of communism as they became obvious midway through the twentieth century. Instead of developing a full-blown existential critique of capitalism, as Marx did, it points to capitalism's moral flaws. Instead of championing wholesale political revolution, as Marx did, modern socialism therefore advocates piecemeal socio-economic reforms.

Bertrand Russell was one humanist who professed such a socialism. He drew a distinction between himself and communists by arguing that following Marx needn't be a 'gospel of proletarian revenge'; it needn't be violent. In his essay, *The Case for Socialism*, he continued:

> ***I regard it primarily as an adjustment to machine production demanded by considerations of common sense, and calculated to increase the happiness, not only of proletarians, but of all except a tiny minority of the human race.***

Russell highlights several flaws in capitalism with which others agreed. They are moral failures in the sense that they are detrimental to human flourishing, at least in a majority of cases. They include:

* Substantial disparities in wealth, opportunities and power between the rich and the poor that creates a permanent underclass, and keeps women and children in subjection.
* Rampant individualism that has no thought for vulnerable members of society, particularly the unemployed or unemployable.

* Leaving the production of all goods and services to market mechanisms in the belief that this turns the market from being a means to deliver these goods and services to being an end in itself; choice and competition come to be seen as virtues in their own right.
* Discrimination against minority groups in society since all people have a right to be part of the society to which they belong.

To these Russell added some other critiques of capitalism that also seem to hold:

* Inequalities in leisure time, since instead of mechanized means of production freeing up time for all to enjoy, it is the capitalist owners who take it at the expense of the workers. He shared this sentiment with Oscar Wilde, who in his essay The Soul of Man under Socialism, opined: 'Cultivated leisure is the aim of man.'
* Poor quality art, since commercial pressures are at odds with artistic expression. Not only does the market more often than not reward poor quality art but it prefers variations on profitable themes not untested departures. Socialism, though, liberates people from these compromises, according to Russell. Again, Wilde concurs when he avers: 'The true artist is a man who believes absolutely in himself, because he is absolutely himself.'
* Russell also believed that the 'unemployed rich' of capitalism were a curse – people with much wealth but little real value to society. The problem is that by virtue of their wealth, they can worm their way into positions of influence though without the moral, intellectual or artistic abilities to exercise that influence well.

As an economic system aimed at achieving better ends, socialists believe in the state ownership of production (to avoid the excesses of the market); the redistribution of wealth (to avoid the creation of an under class); a major role for governments in economic decision-making (to ensure that the market works for people and not people for the market). Economic central planning has also been suggested, though it is arguably more characteristic of communism than socialism.

So where has socialism got to now? Is it a viable option for the contemporary humanist? In the West at least, socialism is nearly as redundant a philosophy as communism. It lost much credibility after the collapse of communism. Critics have also argued that to function properly, socialist policy-makers need to have access to more information about a market than can possibly be provided in any real situation. The resulting lack of information upon which to make decisions only increases amid the dynamism of global markets – militating against the possibility of a successful international socialism, a dream that socialists like Russell shared with Marx. (Russell thought it was the key to ending war.) According to this critique, socialists are, therefore, always condemned to make mistakes, for which the people they would otherwise champion pay the price.

Having said that, social market economics – a sort of compromise between socialism and capitalism – is widespread. It is a set of policies ranging from government funding of a welfare state through to protectionist tax regimes in support of national industries. They are aimed at mitigating the inhumane effects of market forces and providing safety nets for those who would otherwise fall through them.

The origins of utilitarianism

The second of the humanisms for this chapter was founded by Jeremy Bentham (1748–1832), the father of utilitarianism. Bentham was an eighteenth-century English philosopher, very much part of the Enlightenment, who argued that government should aim at the greatest happiness for the greatest number of people. Incidentally, although a contemporary of Thomas Paine, he also thought that the concept of natural rights was a contradiction in terms, calling it 'nonsense on stilts'. However, it was his godson, John Stuart Mill who, a few years after Marx's early work, put together a robust form of utilitarianism that is still highly influential today.

Mill was an extraordinary figure – though he never thought of himself as in any way remarkable. He was learning Greek and maths at the age of three, philosophy and ancient history at six, literature at ten, and economics and logic at 14. Perhaps unsurprisingly, given such a head start, his writings had an enormous impact upon nineteenth-century Britain.

* He was an early advocate of women's rights, writing 'The principle which regulates the existing social relations between the two sexes – the legal subordination of one sex to the other – is wrong in itself, and now one of the chief hindrances to human improvement.'
* Mill also championed liberalism. His formula for what it means to live in a liberal society is still recited. If liberty consists of doing what you desire then it also follows that: 'The liberty of the individual must thus far be limited; he must not make himself a nuisance to other people.' As we saw, he provided a vital rider to Comte's more authoritarian humanism.

His key work on utilitarianism as a theory of ethics came in 1861, with his seminal work on the subject called *Utilitarianism*.

Utility as well-being

Bentham had written that, 'The greatest happiness of the greatest number is the foundation of morals and legislation.' In other words, the word utilitarian refers to those 'utilities' that make life worth living, and utilitarianism is a theory about what people do, how they decide, and how they should act – that is, so as to produce as much well-being as possible.

He then took this logic to its natural conclusion. If the question of life is how to increase the amount of happiness, then this implies a need for a way of measuring the amount of pleasure associated with different kinds of activity. He called this 'felicific calculus'. His aim was to measure the amounts of pleasure for different activities and attach numbers to them. Then people would have a scientific basis upon which to conduct their ethics, simply by choosing the activities that had the highest numbers.

Problems with happiness

At one level, felicific calculus appeals to a natural intuition that we can choose between options on the basis of the pleasure and pain they may cause us. We tend to go for those things that are more pleasurable, and avoid those things that are painful. But when taken as a scientific principle, this hedonism soon runs into absurdities. For example, pleasures come in very different forms. So to compare different pleasures is like comparing the taste of an apple with that of a pear and deciding which is better by asking about the 'appleness' of both. The apple would fare well; the pear not at all. On this scale the pear would not be regarded pleasurable at all. Basically, you cannot compare apples and pears.

Also there is the complicating factor that sometimes pleasures are closely associated with pain. Consider learning to play the piano. The effort it takes a child to bash a melody out on the keys may result in much pain, not only for them but also for their parents. However, the pleasure the child may eventually gain from being able to play later in life could be substantial – though unless they go on to become a concert pianist, the difference between the pleasure and the pain may in retrospect always hang in the balance. But parents, of course, do not decide along these lines at all. Rather they force their children to have lessons because they believe music to be valuable and good.

Mill noticed the problems with utilitarianism as Bentham had formulated it. To those we have just discussed, he added another: 'Ask yourself whether you are happy, and you cease to be so.' In other words, there seemed to be something self-defeating in the very calculated nature of utilitarianism.

But Mill saw something worth rescuing in utilitarianism which led him to write his book. He argued that the problems existed because Bentham had only properly considered one part of life, the empirical, practical part. What had been missed was that human beings also have an emotional life, the side of life that is satisfied by the arts, literature and music.

The key change was the ability to distinguish between higher and lower pleasures. Higher pleasures are things like the arts or friendship. Lower pleasures are things like being fed or keeping warm. This led to another famous observation. In *Utilitarianism*, Mill wrote: 'It is better to be a human being dissatisfied than a pig satisfied; better to be Socrates dissatisfied than a fool satisfied.' What he meant was that a dissatisfied Socrates is a better state to be in than that of a satisfied pig because even with its frustrations, Socrates's life allows him to access higher pleasures. Moreover, even a small taste of the pleasures of such a philosophical life are worth more than being sated on the pleasures of mere consumption.

Contemporary utilitarianism

Mill's reform was the first important one in the history of the idea and, in the intervening years, philosophers have added a number of further refinements. Peter Singer (b. 1946) is one contemporary philosopher closely associated with utilitarianism, being well known for his writing at both a popular and academic level. He has responded to a number of critiques of the theory and is well known for his campaigning work on the welfare of animals. In fact, one of his modifications arises directly from this work. Strictly speaking, utilitarians do not believe in rights since rights imply that there are universal values to which human beings and others should have access. This undermines the notion that it is utility that counts. Singer, though, believes that while establishing the foundations upon which rights might rest is a futile task, the language of human and animal rights is a useful shorthand behind which many of his utilitarian concerns can be addressed and progressed.

He also updates the notion of pleasure and pain with the idea of satisfying preferences. People and animals have preferences that may be natural or, in the case of human beings, rational. And it is the ways in which those preferences can be thwarted that Singer's version of utilitarianism seeks to challenge. For example, an animal has a preference to avoid pain, so that should be the guiding principle in animal husbandry. Alternatively, while a human being might seek to avoid pain, their rational self might calculate that some pains are worth suffering for a greater good. For example, if you go to the dentist you know you might suffer, but you also know that the benefit of having healthy teeth outweighs that temporary setback.

Critics of utilitarianism

So utilitarianism is an active ethical theory today, not least among humanists. However, that is not to say it is without its critics, too. For example, if maximizing happiness is the key imperative then consider the following scenario. Surely, it is better to kill one healthy person, remove their organs, and give them to five or six unhealthy people who would be restored to full, happy lives after the transplants? To put it in utilitarian terms, one person's pain and loss would lead to half a dozen's pleasure and gain. We intuitively react against this thought, but within the parameters of its own theory, utilitarianism appears to find it difficult to say why we should not act in this way.

Similarly, consider the issue of torture. Surely, utilitarianism would suggest that it is better to torture one individual who might have information about some pending atrocity, than risk hundreds of people's lives who might be saved? Again, there is something about torture that seems fundamentally wrong. It is just that utilitarianism doesn't help us identify what it is.

Life in the round

The utilitarians have responded to these problems by saying both scenarios represent immoral acts because of the effect they have on others. In the case of the transplants, the practice of killing healthy people would cause very many people to worry that they might be next, so it would actually increase unhappiness in the general population. Similarly, the practice of torture should cause widespread discontent because it is such a hideous thing to do.

There is a further point that follows from these ripostes. When thinking about what makes life worthwhile, we do not actually consider what makes us happy by examining our various activities in isolation and then only doing those that carry some pleasure. Life is more connected than that. For example, going to work is an activity that includes both happy-making things, like being paid or finding friends, and unhappy-making things, like having to sit in an office or stand in a factory for hours on end. The two aspects, though, are two sides of the same coin. What we need to do is consider life in the round, in its whole context.

This thought has led some utilitarians to the paradoxical conclusion that the best way to live as a utilitarian – that is to maximize well-being in the world – is actually not to make the calculations that would otherwise seem to be characteristic of utilitarianism. Rather, it is better to follow your common sense for most of the time, and only resort to utilitarian decision-making in extreme situations. This has been called rule utilitarianism – the conviction that for most of the time it is better to follow moral rules, only breaking them when the consequences would clearly be bad.

On why bad things lead to worse

However, another philosopher, Bernard Williams (1929–2003), has pursued this paradox further and identified a more profound problem with utilitarianism.

Williams argued that the problem with utilitarianism is that it treats people instrumentally. They become objects of the theory's calculations, and so serve those calculations, rather than being treated as human individuals in their own right. This is why utilitarianism finds it hard to answer why a healthy person should not donate their organs and, similarly, why one person should not be tortured. If it had a conception of each and every human being as an end in themselves, and not as a means to other ends, even other human ends, then it could reject these cases with force.

If you want an example of this tragic outcome then you need look no further than the Iraq war of 2003. Proponents of the war made a utilitarian case for it. They argued that while war itself is a bad thing, it would lead to the greater good of freeing the people of Iraq to live democratically. However, war itself unleashes resentment, revenge and rage, so the successive bad things that must be done to combat the realities of the war came to swamp any good that the initial aggression might have provided.

Having noted the critiques, there are a number of features of utilitarianism that its proponents continue to find compelling. Humanists in particular are drawn by a number of core elements:

* The clarity of the theory.
* It is down to earth and very practical.
* It is not reliant on religious traditions or belief in an absolute good or evil.
* It does not depend on obeying the rules of any received authority.
* It strives to reduce the amount of pain in the world, as much as increase the pleasures of life.

* By focusing on reducing suffering as the central moral task, it is able to embrace concerns about the well-being of animals as well as humans.
* It incorporates a sense that progress can be made in ethics and in terms of improving people's lives.
* It is amenable to scientific interpretation.

Since these elements are key starting points in moral philosophy for many humanists, utilitarianism is always likely to be held in high regard.

Pragmatism

It has often been noticed that there is something quite European, even English, about utilitarianism. It advocates moderation in thought and a focus on the happy, contented life. It is as if it suits many of the intellectual tastes and national characteristics found on the eastern coast of the Atlantic.

The third of our humanistic philosophies in this chapter, pragmatism, has been called the American philosophy. There is something in its focus on what works, in its synthesis of the practical and philosophical, that chimes with the 'just do it' element in the American character. It is even quite accommodating of religion, the revivalist feature of life on the other side of the Atlantic that is often so incomprehensible to European humanists. It has had a distinguished history throughout the twentieth century, and into the twenty-first, particularly in America. It is still a lively strand within humanism today.

The person who first popularized it, and thereby provides a way into it for us, was William James (1842–1910). James was a likeable man; his success as a philosopher in his own lifetime was as much due to his character as his thought. In his *History of Western Philosophy*, Bertrand Russell notes that James was almost universally loved:

> ***On the scientific side, the study of medicine had given his thoughts a tendency towards***

materialism, which, however, was held in check by his religious emotions. His religious feelings were very Protestant, very democratic, and very full of the warmth of human kindness. He refused altogether to follow his brother Henry into fastidious snobbishness.

Philosophically, James's thought can be broken down into three tenets. First, his beliefs about subjectivity and objectivity; second, his thoughts about what it is to take a decision when it comes to believing in something; and third, his adherence to the so-called principle of pragmatism.

1 **Any radical distinction between subject and object is false.** This first tenet is perhaps the most difficult to understand. For example, it seems natural to assume that someone knows something – the 'someone' being the subject, the 'something' being the object that they know. James argued this is illusion. The reason is that there can be no radical difference between mind (subject) and matter (object); rather, all the world is made up of the same stuff which James called 'pure experience'. Those who say that mind is different from matter 'are clinging to a mere echo, the faint rumour left behind by the disappearing "soul" upon the air of philosophy'. This disappearance of the soul might appeal to humanist sensibilities. But the necessity of denying any radical distinction between subject and object brings problems with it. For example, what might 'pure experience' itself be? It is an idea that many philosophers since James have found unsatisfactory.

2 **We often have to make decisions about beliefs** for which there are inadequate rational grounds. If the first tenet is difficult, the second is more straightforward. For it is surely the case that in practice, we often have

to make decisions about beliefs for which there are inadequate rational grounds. James called it the 'Will to Believe', in an essay of the same title. He thought that religious belief was the quintessential example. For example, a sceptic may decide that they cannot believe in God, not because the evidence is against deities, but because having concluded that the evidence alone is not enough to decide one way or another, they would rather avoid the error of believing in God when it might well not be true. According to James, though, the religious believer may also conclude that though the evidence is inadequate, there is a duty to believe in truth as much as there is to shun error. This first imperative is what the sceptic ignores at the risk of not believing something that is in fact true. Of course, both the believer and the sceptic may be duped. But James suggests that being duped 'through hope' is better than being duped 'through fear'.

The weakness of this tenet is that it doesn't take much account of the probability of whether things may or may not exist. So, someone may think that it is overwhelmingly unlikely that God exists and so call themselves an atheist. It is not so much that they fear committing what they regard as the error of theism as simply that they regard theism itself as enormously improbable. (Whether or not God can be judged to exist as a question of probability is another question entirely.)

3 **Something can be said to be true if it works – that is, if it has the virtue of making people happy.** This is called the principle of pragmatism. It can be summarized by saying that the value of a theory is not primarily whether or not it is true, but whether it works. James wrote: 'We cannot reject any hypothesis if consequences useful to life flow from it.' And even more strongly: 'The true is the name of whatever proves itself to be good in the way of belief.'

This relationship between truth and utility needs clarification. For example, it might be thought to imply that truth simply does not matter; even that it doesn't exist. James denied such nihilism. Instead, he argued that if something worked for him then it was not just true but was truth. Conversely, he sought to draw a different kind of distinction, namely that truth is not the same as reality. 'Realities are not *true*, they *are*; and beliefs are true *of* them.'

Problems with 'what works'

A number of difficulties are raised by James's pragmatism. Bertrand Russell rejected it on several grounds:

1 **The difficulty of saying what is good.** Russell argued that to apply the principle of pragmatism you must first arrive at a true idea of what is good, which is notoriously hard to do. (The situation for pragmatists seems even more complicated, Russell continued, if for them the truth of something is already intimately related to its goodness – which is tantamount to tautology, arguing that what is good is good because it is good.) James, though, could reply that much of the difficulty of deciding what is good stems from the presumed need to have an objective account of it. Subjectively speaking, this is not necessarily hard at all. And he has already denied the difference between the two.

2 **The fact that some truths do not depend upon their efficacy.** Russell argued that some things simply are true, notably historical facts such as that Columbus sailed across the Atlantic in 1492. The idea that the truth of this dating depends upon whether or not it is good for humanity is clearly ridiculous. However, I think that James escapes this ridicule since his pragmatism is directed at truths for which there isn't enough evidence in principle to decide. This is not the case for historical facts where there is evidence.

3 The accusation that it avoids certain fundamental questions. Russell argued that when applied to religion, pragmatism avoids fundamental theological questions, such as whether God is, or is not, actually in heaven. For James, though, this thought would be a prime case in which there is not enough evidence upon which to make an objective decision.

4 It tries to circumvent fundamental scepticism. Finally, Russell argues that, 'James's doctrine is an attempt to build a superstructure of belief upon a foundation of scepticism, and like all such attempts it is dependent on fallacies.' In relation to religion, Russell's accusation is that for most believers, who are by definition not sceptics, the correct thing to say about their convictions is, 'I believe in God and therefore I am happy.' James, though, reinterprets the believer's faith, converting it into the statement, 'If I believed in God I would be happy; therefore, I believe in God.' Little wonder, Russell notes, that the Pope condemned pragmatism. In short, you cannot have your sceptical cake and eat it.

The priority of experience in religion

As an aside, I am not sure this is what James is saying of belief at all. Rather, in his most important book, *The Varieties of Religious Experience*, he is asking what it means to have a religious experience. In other words, James realizes that what primarily counts in religion is not the *belief* but the *experience* – the felt difference it makes. This is the basis of its cognitive significance. So people's interpretations of their religious experiences form the primary material for the study of religion, even when supplementary explanations of these experiences are subsequently offered. Religious feelings and impulses are not as calculating as Russell suggests.

Therefore Russell's accusation – that James advocates the justification of religious belief because of its utility – makes the mistake of giving priority to the religious belief. Rather, *belief* comes after; it tries to make sense of the *experience*. Incidentally, this is something that all religious institutions, such as churches, understand if only by their failure to keep a cap on what people make of their experiences: it is for this reason that heterodoxy and heresy are at least as resilient as orthodoxy.

Incidentally, a related and important fact that James draws attention to, even in the title of his book, is that religious experience is nothing if not various. It cannot simply be equated with a peak experience, or a sense of connectedness, or a creative urge, or a loss of self, or a feeling of bliss. At different times, religious people have said it is all these things and none of them.

Ignoring or forgetting this is the mistake that James's successors, present-day neuropsychologists of religion, often appear to make. They seek physiological explanations for religion, typically by monitoring activity in the brain, and thereby assume it is one thing or the other, normally some kind of peak or exceptional experience.

Pragmatism as a humanism

Explicit links between pragmatism and humanism were not championed until a generation after James, notably by the philosopher F. C. S. Schiller (1864–1937). Schiller made the connections explicit in his book *Humanism: Philosophical Essays*, published in 1903. His version of humanism is based upon pragmatism and, in particular, the notion that for something to be true it must at least have some practical application in life. In fact, positive practicality is key to something being thought of as humanistic. Schiller is also at pains to show what a waste of valuable philosophical time, as it were, it has been to speculate on intellectual matters that can have no possible bearing upon what works. He wants to show that wordy metaphysics is pointless unless its meaning has some application and its thought some purpose.

Other pragmatists

Dewey

Another pragmatist and contemporary of Schiller – and someone who, philosophically speaking, is more important – was the American John Dewey (1859–1952). Bertrand Russell thought Dewey the most distinguished living philosopher at the time. Dewey sought to turn pragmatism into a systematic theory. He did so by rejecting all dualisms – mind/body, fact/value, means/ends – and by developing his pragmatism on evolutionary principles: he envisaged philosophy as a continually self-correcting process, not unlike evolutionary change. He also thought that philosophy makes progress like science, though is limited in the sense that this progress is only ever in relation to current experience. In fact, he was an advocate of what is called 'fallibilism', the view that no fact, rule or idea is ever certain. This means that philosophy differs from science on two counts:

1. **Experience** It embraces a wider range of experiences than science can, including moral and aesthetic dimensions of existence in particular.
2. **Truth** It is also different in terms of its understanding of truth. Dewey wrote: 'Truth is the opinion which is fated to be ultimately agreed to by all who investigate' – showing his indebtedness to the pragmatic principle. In other words, truth is judged by its effects.

It should also be added that Dewey has been an inspiration to some humanists for his contribution to society at large, particularly for his tireless work in the sphere of education.

Rorty

To bring our account of pragmatism up to date, we should mention a philosopher who died recently, namely Richard Rorty (1931–2007). He was another pragmatist advocate of deflationary accounts of truth – offending many when he argued that most of philosophy since Plato has been interesting but useless. He preferred philosophy that contributed to a wider conversation between human beings on justice and truth without worrying about the grounds for justice and truth: it would aim at accounts that work in terms of delivering practical goods. 'Time will tell, but epistemology won't,' he wrote in one book. To put it another way, he saw philosophy as an essentially creative and imaginative exercise.

It is also a collective one, since the greatest utility philosophy might have – its aim therefore – is solidarity. He wrote:

> ***If we could be moved solely by the desire for solidarity, setting aside the desire for objectivity altogether, then we should think of human progress as making it possible for human beings to do more interesting things and be more interesting people, not as heading towards a place which has somehow been prepared for us in advance.***

This vision is clearly humanistic, being focused on the betterment of human beings. However, Rorty found himself at odds with other humanists, even those who could be called pragmatic. For example, he might be thought naïve in thinking that human beings can simply give up their longing to find things that are true with a capital 'T'. Critics of Rorty might reply that Plato has lasted for a very good reason: he is not just creative and imaginative but aims to be right. Also, there are many humanists who could not or would not give up on all objective criteria for truth, no matter how hard they might be to ascertain.

Summary

In this chapter, we have examined three major humanistic philosophies from the modern period when thinkers began to call themselves humanists. However, we have also seen that what humanism might be can vary radically. We have considered three versions here.

* The first was an approach to humanism inspired by Marx which majors on the belief that philosophy must not focus on the individual, or only on the individual, but on the social. It is arguably the least important kind of humanism in operation today, though still carries some weight in social economics.
* The second was utilitarianism, an ethical approach to humanism which seeks to maximize the greatest happiness for the greatest number. It gained great weight in the form developed by Mill and, in the philosophies of utilitarians like Peter Singer, is a major force among humanist thinkers today.
* The third humanism was pragmatism. Summed up as 'what works', it too has developed into a major strand within humanism, appealing particularly to those who believe that the old aims of philosophy, to ascertain what is true, are less important than developing ways of thinking that better allow humans to live together.

Before leaving this chapter, it is worth just referring to two other kinds of humanism that relate to those we have encountered.

Literary humanism

Literary humanism, also call the New Humanism, was a literary movement that emerged in the early decades of the twentieth century, soon after pragmatism. It argued that human beings are unique in the natural world, that experience is fundamentally moral not natural, and that human beings are free, though subject to natural laws. An important advocate was Matthew Arnold, who wrote books including *Culture and Anarchy* (1869) and *Essays in Criticism* (1888). He looked back to writers like Chaucer who he believed had gained 'the power to survey the world from a central, a truly human point of view'. For Arnold, Chaucer was the first to explore everyday experience, as opposed to that of the clergy or aristocracy. Added to this, Chaucer, though a great poet, had the virtue of being an ordinary human being too – an observation that celebrates the uniqueness *and* universality of the human condition.

Feminism

A second kind of humanism can be linked to Marxism, and is based upon feminist philosophy. It can be linked to Marxism inasmuch as if Marx had critiqued the individualistic line of thought from the Enlightenment, then feminists critiqued the fact that it was not just individualistic but decidedly male too. Feminism has developed into a broad philosophical movement that it is not possible to do justice to here. However, broadly speaking, it seeks both to establish equality for women and to understand the patriarchal roots of culture and thought.

For humanists, a key feminist issue is that of the traditional association between women and irrationality, which if humanism stresses the rational nature of Man [sic], can perpetuate patriarchal patterns of thought. Similarly, a humanism that stresses the 'human animal's' place in nature can also import a social determinism which ascribes particular roles to women, curtailing their freedom. Much has been written on feminism and some seminal texts include Mary Wollstonecraft's *A Vindication of the Rights of Women* (1792), John Stuart Mill's *The Subjection of Women* (1869) and Carol Gilligan's *In a Different Voice* (1982).

In relation to feminism, an interesting conundrum for humanists today is the wearing of the veil by Muslim women. These women claim it as their right, arguing that it is a sign of respect and honour. They sound almost like feminists in so doing. Humanists, though, will see the veil as symbolic of a repressive religious social order and want to reject it.

2

existential questions and doubts

We come now to another humanist philosophy of the twentieth century, existentialism. Its key principle is that we humans are freer than we know, and it is up to human individuals to seize the chance at learning to live well, by creating a sense of meaning. That said, existentialism also recognizes that such freedom can be daunting, provoking anxiety.

We then turn to what are sometimes referred to as anti-humanist philosophies, though they are important for their doubts: their ideas can be valuable to humanists because they are 'masters of suspicion', and so teach scepticism, a key humanist value.

First, there's Friedrich Nietzsche, who announced the death of God. Then, there's Michel Foucault, who warned that if you get rid of God, you might put man in God's place.

In the twentieth century the humanist philosophies of the nineteenth century, notably utilitarianism and Marxism, were sustained, developed and often enriched. There was also the American invention of pragmatism. However, that was not the only humanist innovation of the twentieth century. In continental Europe two more important developments emerged. The first is existentialism, the philosophy that acclaims the absolute freedom of the human individual. The second is sometimes called anti-humanism, though I shall argue it has a proper place within the history of humanism because it offers criticisms of humanism that are important to engage with. It is to these strands that we now turn.

Radical freedom

Strictly speaking, existentialism is a philosophy whose roots reach back into the nineteenth century. The Danish philosopher Søren Kierkegaard (1813–55) is usually identified as its founder. He argued that the subjective, personal dimension of life is what matters. 'What use would it be if I were to discover so-called objective truth?' he asked in his journal. 'The thing is to find a truth which is truth for me, to find the idea for which I am willing to live and die.' It is this subjectivity that became central to existentialism.

With this human centeredness, one can see the immediate appeal of existentialism as a form of humanism. However, it was not until the twentieth century and the existentialism of Jean-Paul Sartre (1905–80), that it became explicitly identified with humanism. Sartre was famous in France and the world over as a novelist, playwright and philosopher. He was also awarded the Nobel Prize for Literature in 1964, though he declined it. However, his importance to humanism can be focused on a lecture he gave in 1946. It was entitled *Existentialism is a Humanism* and has become another seminal text in the history of humanism.

Sartre begins by identifying various charges that, at the time, had been laid against existentialism:

* It had been accused of being quietist; encouraging people to contemplate their existence, not act to improve it.
* It was accused of being ignominious and individualistic – the first because it dwells on the darker side of life, the second because it begins with Descartes' famous 'I think therefore I am', a solitary account of humankind.
* It was accused of being anarchic, propagating a moral code of 'each to their own'.

It is to combat these charges of pathetic inaction, dismal pessimism and dangerous solipsism that he appeals to the word humanism. No small part of the problem, Sartre continued, is that existentialism as a philosophy has come to mean everything and nothing; it has become a victim of its own success, used almost synonymously with words like 'expressive' or alternatively in wholly alien contexts such as 'existential crisis'.

So what does Sartre think humanism can deliver, and what does existentialism mean to him? In a word, freedom. And this is what people find so alarming about existentialism: 'It confronts man with a possibility of choice.' To put it in a more technical way, what lies at the heart of existentialism is the belief that 'existence comes before *essence*' – that is, when thinking about what it is to be human, existentialists begin with the subjective experience of being human, not some kind of objective understanding of human nature. 'We mean that man first of all exists, encounters himself, surges up in the world – and defines himself afterwards ... and then he will be what he makes of himself.'

Dignity as self-determination

Sartre calls this capacity for self-realization the first principle of existentialism. Therein lies the dignity of humankind

– that long-standing theme within humanism – for it distinguishes people from mere things. 'Man is, before all else, something which propels itself towards a future and is aware that it is doing so.' Various things follow from this dignity:

* With it comes a tremendous personal responsibility. If every person is capable of self-realization then the onus for doing so rests squarely upon each person's shoulders.
* With it also comes a tremendous collective responsibility. For when one person defines themselves, they also define what it is to be human and this has some kind of impact upon all other humans' sense of themselves. Thus, the image that we fashion for ourselves 'is valid for all and for the entire epoch in which we find ourselves'.

It is because of this collective responsibility that many of the supposedly pessimistic characteristics of existentialism follow. Take anguish: this is the burden of asking what might happen if everyone did as you yourself are now doing. It is the concern that every leader understands. For what that means is this:

> ***If I regard a certain course of action as good, it is only I who can choose to say that it is good and not bad ... Everything happens to every man as though the whole human race had its eyes fixed upon what he is doing and regulated its conduct accordingly.***

Abandonment

Another key word for Sartre is abandonment. This refers to his atheism and the desire to understand the consequences of the non-existence of God 'right to the end'. He thinks this is important since if the ramifications of a Godless universe are avoided or finessed in some way then this denial threatens the very foundations of morality. In other words, the existentialist understands very well that with the disappearance of God also disappears the possibility of locating human values in some transcendent realm. 'It is nowhere written that "the good" exists, that one must be honest or must not lie, since we are now upon the plane where there are only men.'

One thing to note about Sartre's atheism is that it is not obsessed with showing that God does not exist. Towards the end of *Existentialism is a Humanism*, Sartre says:

> ***Existentialism is not atheist in the sense that it would exhaust itself in demonstrations of the non-existence of God. It declares, rather, that even if God existed that would make no difference from its point of view. Not that we believe God does exist, but we think that the real problem is not that of His existence; what man needs is to find himself again and to understand that nothing can save him from himself, not even a valid proof of the existence of God.***

This, Sartre explains, is what he means when he says that people are *condemned* to be free. We did not create ourselves but upon finding ourselves thrown into the world, we are at liberty. And this liberty is frightening because there are no rules as to how we should live; no commandments that can tell us what to do.

Worse still, we cannot turn in on ourselves to find our 'true' selves and then try to realize that. People are not born heroes, they make themselves heroes. People are not born cowards, their cowardice is their responsibility. Sartre states: 'I can neither seek within myself for an authentic impulse to action, nor can I expect, from some ethic, formulae that will enable me to act.' So we are abandoned to decide what to do for ourselves, to work out how to be. It is another source of liberative anguish. Sartre continues:

> ***This is humanism, because we remind man that there is no legislator but himself; that he himself, thus abandoned, must decide for himself; also because we show that it is not by turning back upon himself, but always by seeking, beyond himself, an aim which is one of liberation or of some particular realization, that man can realize himself as truly human.***

Action

Such thoughts might lead to despair, to the pessimism that his accusers level against him. However, Sartre argues the opposite. It means, for example, that if someone has been cowardly, then they are also always free to be heroic now. If someone has been a liar, they can start to speak truthfully. Conversely, someone else who refuses to be free, say, by arguing that they are following an authority like the Church or that their actions are determined by some imagined inner nature, are susceptible to the existentialist's judgement: they are cowards.

Sartre cannot have hope for the future of humankind because he does not believe there is any natural goodness within human beings that will automatically win out. However, because he as one person can choose to do good, at least as he sees it, he can work fiercely for a better tomorrow. This is why existentialism is not quietist. Quite the opposite: properly understood it leads to action. In fact, without action, human beings are nothing. Sartre states: 'Man is nothing else but what he purposes, he exists only in so far as he realizes himself, he is therefore nothing else but the sum of his actions, nothing else but what his life is.'

Moreover, because every other individual is in the same boat as I am, they become invaluable sources for understanding my own predicament, and I theirs. 'The other is indispensable to my existence, and equally so too any knowledge I can have of myself.' The truth of this is reinforced because although there is no essential human nature, there are very widespread conditions of human existence in which people live. For example, the time in which someone is born will decide whether they are a slave, a baron or a proletarian. And that will be the same for everyone else born in that time. This again is a source of solidarity.

Existentialism rebuts the charge of relativism with a similar line of thought. Sartre admits that it is the case that existentialists do not have any universal maxims or conception of morality like, say, Kant did. However, he also thinks that such universals are more or less useless in practice, since in practice, ethics is always particular, always specific.

Problems with existential humanism

Sartre's account of existentialism as a humanism therefore has many qualities that other humanists would admire: the dignity of humanity; the freedom to choose; the sense of connection with others; the seriousness of its moral purpose and so on. However, there are some facets that are more problematic:

1 Anti-essentialism

Perhaps the most fundamental issue concerns Sartre's anti-essentialism. He explicitly denies that human beings should be regarded as of supreme value. There is no essence of humanity to which human beings must return or be resolved towards. Humanity, as opposed to individual human beings, cannot be an end in itself, for human beings must define themselves.

Elsewhere, Sartre had ridiculed even the possibility. He says it is absurd to declare 'Man is magnificent!' simply because, say, we can build aeroplanes that fly higher than mountains. It would make equal sense to conclude that the mountains are magnificent and human beings are poor flying creatures like gnats.

Sartre also points out that there is a grave danger in essentialist conceptions of humanism. They result in all sorts of crimes being committed against actual groups or individuals in the name of an oppressive ideal of humanity that finds certain groups or individuals marred or polluting. Nazism obviously comes to mind, though in *Existentialism is a Humanism*, Sartre continues:

> ***And we have no right to believe that humanity is something to which we could set up a cult, after the manner of Auguste Comte. The cult of humanity ends in Comtian humanism, shut-in upon itself, and – this must be said – in Fascism. We do not want humanism like that.***

2 Atheism

Sartre's humanism is fundamentally atheistic. In fact, he believes it is theism that has encouraged people to make the mistake of putting essence before existence. This is based upon the myth that God designed human beings before creating them. 'The conception of man in the mind of God is comparable to that of the paper-knife in the mind of the artisan: God makes man according to a procedure and a conception, exactly as the artisan manufactures a paper-knife, following a definition and formula.'

A similar notion is found buried in the humanistic essentialism of the eighteenth century. There, the belief in God may be wholly or partially suppressed. And yet the concept of

religion, it is not as if they had much of an alternative but to stick with humanism in some shape or form.

Here, we will discuss in detail just two figures, Friedrich Nietzsche (1844–1900) and Michel Foucault (1926–84). Their aim was radical: to reinvigorate humanist ideas and rid them of faults or weaknesses. In other words, they are the inheritors of the sceptical tradition that reaches back through the eighteenth century in the work of Kant and Hume, and to the Renaissance in the writing of Montaigne and Machiavelli. Indeed, both Foucault and Nietzsche have been called 'Masters of Suspicion'.

Friedrich Nietzsche

Nietzsche provides a good place to start, not least because it was he who proclaimed what many people at the time were thinking: God is dead. However, before coming to that let us first consider some of the other elements that he denounced at the same time. It is these that give rise to the anti-humanist accusation.

First, Nietzsche loathed Christianity. This might be thought the mark of a good humanist by some, not an anti-humanist, but it was the way in which Nietzsche denounced Christianity that can disturb even an atheistic humanist. He argued that Christianity encourages a slave mentality. This is partly because of the necessity of submitting to a deity, but also because of Christianity's ethical requirement to serve others. Nietzsche thought this dehumanizing. For example, to have pity on others is patronizing to them and self-indulgent of you. He wrote in *The Gay Science*:

> ***When we see somebody suffer, we like to exploit this opportunity to take possession of him; those who become his benefactors and pity him, for example, do this and call the lust for a new possession that he***

awakens in them 'love'; and the pleasure they feel is comparable to that aroused by the prospect of a new conquest.

Instead, Nietzsche encouraged people to rejoice together even in the midst of suffering. This, though, runs the risk of appearing inhumane. It might challenge the humanist virtues of solidarity and fellow-feeling.

Questioning progress

Second, Nietzsche attacked scientific progressivism, the notion that through science, human knowledge advances and progresses. This seems like a more direct attack on humanism. Nietzsche identified three phases through which this positivist doctrine has passed since the advent of modern science.

* The first was that of Newton, who believed that science would reveal the goodness and wisdom of God. As an atheist, Nietzsche thought this self-evidently untrue.
* The second was that of Voltaire, who believed that science would elicit knowledge that would improve human morality and happiness. This might have been possible to believe in the eighteenth century, but no more.
* The third is perhaps typical of many scientists now who see their discipline as the pursuit of objective, disinterested knowledge, and not tainted with the flaws of most other disciplines. This, though, becomes unsustainable, according to Nietzsche, as soon as you observe the processes of science, which are driven by competition and power. Further, a little philosophy of science, drawing on the work of someone like Hume, shows that science rapidly loses any easy claim to objectivity.

So, Nietzsche thought that all three positivist attitudes to science were based on fundamental errors.

Historical perspectivism

The examples above point to more profound critiques that Nietzsche had of humanism. For example, he thought it lacked a proper historical sense, which might manifest itself in a number of ways. The doctrine of progress is one, in that it fails to see both that it has been undermined before and that its origins are possibly quite unpalatable to its contemporary adherents. Philosophically speaking, a related but more substantial complaint is that the moral virtues held by humanism are themselves historically conditioned.

Consider the dignity of humankind. Pico, the author of the phrase, appears to have located man's dignity in occult knowledge that would enable him to become divine. The eighteenth-century humanists saw man's dignity in a kind of post-Christian understanding of humankind as the pinnacle of creation. This was dashed with the discovery of evolution, but was reinvented again in the twentieth century by conceptions of dignity as freedom or spirit. Nietzsche's point is that a value like dignity depends on your historic time and place. This doctrine is sometimes called 'perspectivism'. Without this sense of time and place, Nietzsche would say that championing man's dignity becomes empty rhetoric.

Character and dignity

This, in turn, matters because empty rhetoric is corrosive. It lacks honesty. It corrals human beings as herd-like animals rather than cultivating their individual dignity. In *The Gay Science*, one of the books of Nietzsche's so-called middle period, when these themes are articulated very accessibly, he writes of one thing that is needful for the modern individual, that is, 'To "give style" to one's character – a great and rare art!' What Nietzsche argues is that the dignified individual is one who can turn an eye on themselves and survey their weaknesses and strengths. Both facets, once admitted and understood, can be knitted together to form one's character, to lend it style. It takes a long time and much practice, but these are admirable people. They find satisfaction in life. They are able to throw off the resentment of those who do not have the courage to examine themselves. For such resentment, with its desire for revenge, makes for the most undignified of human creatures.

The death of God

Nowhere is this courageousness more needed than in Nietzsche's exploration of what it means to live in an age without God. Nietzsche makes his announcement of the death of God in a rather unexpected way. He tells the story of a madman who one day went to the marketplace. His fellow human beings were about their everyday, secular activities – living already in an age that had left God behind. And the madman cried out: 'I seek God! I seek God!' They laughed and mocked, asking whether God had got lost, or whether God is hiding, or if God is afraid of us? But then the madman turns on his tormenters. 'I will tell you,' he cries. 'We have killed him – you and I.'

Nietzsche's point is not to plead God's cause; rather it is to indicate the ramifications of God's departure from the modern world. They are not unlike the way the world shatters when someone is murdered. The madman continues his articulation of this horrifying state of affairs in cosmological terms:

> ***How could we drink up the sea? Who gave us the sponge to wipe away the entire horizon? What were we doing when we unchained this earth from its sun? Whither is it moving now? Whither are we moving? Away from all suns? Are we not plunging continually? Backward, sideward, forward, in all directions? Is there still any up or***

down? Are we not straying as through an infinite nothing? Do we not feel the breath of empty space? Has it not become colder? Is not night continually closing in on us?

And so the 'madman' continues, for he is not really mad but a prophet. He understands the atheistic human condition more clearly than those around him. It may have been inevitable that God died. It may have been desirable. Presumably Nietzsche thought so, as an atheist.

The disillusionment of Enlightenment

This, then, is another of Nietzsche's criticisms of humanism. Its atheism – or at least its sense of having moved beyond the superstitions of our medieval forbears – can be so glib; as if all that is required is to breathe deeply of Enlightenment air and watch as the sun dispels the clouds! The humanist call, as Nietzsche sees it, is actually far more tremendous than that. Nietzsche is rehearsing the warning of Kant, that Enlightenment is tough, that in political revolutions and personal delusions it can go wrong. It would be better to say this was an age of Enlightenment rather than an enlightened age.

Later in *The Gay Science*, Nietzsche offers his own estimation of how long Enlightenment might take. Centuries, he muses. And in the meantime, human beings will be constantly tempted to fall back on old superstitions and old faiths, often without even realizing it. Chief among these will be the conviction that they are enlightened already.

Michel Foucault *

Michel Foucault is another philosopher frequently tarred with the anti-humanist brush, because he takes issue with rigid conceptions of 'man'. Foucault objects to this essentialism because he believes it is actually constructed – constructed through various discourses, of ambiguous benefit to actual human beings, which developed in the modern period. For example, psychiatric discourses constructed increasingly complex ideas of what it is to be mad and what it is to be sane. Legal discourses did the same in terms of what it is to be criminal and law-abiding. Moral discourses constructed ideas of what it is to be deviant and normal.

The reason these discourses are of ambiguous benefit is that real people fall across the categories they create – perhaps being somewhat mad and somewhat sane, somewhat deviant and somewhat normal. The robust idea of 'man' disciplines us into normative behaviour, so that we might think of ourselves as sane, law-abiding, normal individuals. And for many, much of the time, that is fine. However, those who fall outside of the boundaries – the mad, criminal deviants – are more fiercely disciplined, propelled to the margins of society by modern institutions like the penal system, and held in other modern institutions like the psychiatric hospital.

A recent invention

It is this legacy of eighteenth- and nineteenth-century humanism to which Foucault objects. In a famous passage at the conclusion of his book, *The Order of Things*, he writes:

> ***One thing in any case is certain: man is neither the oldest nor the most constant problem that has been posed for human knowledge. Taking a relatively short chronological sample within a restricted geographical area – European culture since the sixteenth century – one can be certain that man is a recent invention within it ... As the archaeology of our thought easily shows, man is an invention of recent date. And one perhaps nearing its end.***

It is this talk of man being a 'recent invention' that annoys some humanists. It questions essentialist understandings of human nature, like those of Rousseau that argue for an innocent 'state-of-nature' lying underneath the corruptions brought about by living in society.

Power-knowledge

Foucault's phrase for this was 'power-knowledge'. It aims to capture the sense in which any claim to have knowledge about people, such as that they are mad or deviant, also entails an exercise of power over them. So someone who is declared mad can be locked up in the madhouse. Someone who is found guilty can be incarcerated in a prison. Obviously, there is some reason to do this, some good that might result. But it is deluded of the champions of progress to presume that the good of humanity is the only result.

The insane become institutionalized and may never be capable of living in the wider world again. Are they better or worse off for that? It is a question that must be asked, in the name of humanity. Similarly, the imprisoned may be led into a life of crime by being locked up. Indeed the chances are that they will be, if the evidence of organizations like the Howard League for Penal Reform is anything to go by. In a typically strident phrase Foucault concludes that: 'Humanity installs each of its violences in a system of rules and thus proceeds from domination to domination.'

So is there any chance of a philosophy of humanism with a hope that things can get better? Foucault asked this question by asking one that had been asked by Kant: what is Enlightenment? His essay of that title was published in the year Foucault died, suddenly and as a relatively young man. It is perhaps for this reason that it is often overlooked, but to my mind humanists would find much in it to inspire them.

Questioning yourself

Foucault turns back to Kant's answer and assesses it. He writes: 'Kant, in fact, describes Enlightenment as the moment when humanity is going to put its own reason to use, without subjecting itself to any authority.' From this follows Kant's project of critique which Foucault thinks is interesting because it is a self-critique: Kant tries to reflect upon 'the contemporary status of his own enterprise'. He questions himself. He tries to understand what is different about his own philosophy and where it might fall short. This becomes a 'practice of liberty' because it also seeks to transcend the limitations of what our generation has received, notably the neat divisions between the normal and deviant. And this can be thought of as a creative task, one even of invention.

Coming out

A useful case in point is one that was close to Foucault himself, namely that of sexuality. Foucault was homosexual – a category of human sexuality that has only existed since the nineteenth century. This is not, of course, to suggest that there were no men who loved men, and no men who had sex with other men, before then. Rather it is to point out that understanding oneself as *a* homosexual is a recent conception. The Ancient Greek man who had a relationship with another man did not think of himself as different from other men, as the contemporary gay person does, at least to some degree.

Now, this modern turn has brought about many benefits for gay people, from gay bars to civil partnerships. However, Foucault also believed they come at a price, namely the risk of categorizing yourself as a gay man or woman, as if that were somehow a defining feature of yourself. This is to enjoy a freedom – the freedom to be gay – by imposing a kind of limit upon yourself. So, Foucault argued, the real goal of gay liberation should not be just to 'come out' but ultimately to find a 'way out' of the business of calling people gay or straight altogether – that would be truly liberated. He hoped that was happening, and it was part of what he meant when he wrote that man was a recent invention and perhaps nearing its end.

Summary

There are other figures we could point to that have been thought anti-humanist. Sigmund Freud (1856–1939) would be one, the inventor of psychoanalysis, as well as interpreter of dreams, 'discoverer' of the unconscious and brilliant essayist. The paradox is that although Freud can be a figure of hate and ridicule among humanists, and his work branded a pseudo-science, he saw himself as an 'Enlightener', a rationalist who sought to throw light into the darkest corners of the human mind.

The same would be true of the other 'anti-humanists'. They were masters of suspicion because they sought to leave their fellows less deluded. For Nietzsche, this meant trying to see things in an historical perspective and realizing that the death of God did not imply any automatic liberation, any more than simply heralding an age as one of enlightenment meant that the people in it were enlightened. For Foucault, a crucial issue is to understand that progress is not always what it seems to be. Moreover, while humanists quite rightly seek knowledge, they might also be aware that what they believe to be true has ramifications for others that can actually be oppressive.

These are all useful critiques of humanism. To my mind, they have as much of a place in the recent history of humanism as the more straightforwardly positive doctrines of utilitarianism, pragmatism and the other humanism we have introduced in this chapter, namely existentialism – the humanism that advocates freedom.

3

humanisms, religious and secular

No book on humanism would be complete without an exploration of the Darwinian revolution, which offers a naturalistic explanation for the apparent design of life in the world. That said, Darwinism is not necessarily against religious belief, though many believers have been challenged by it.

There is a fascinating parallel struggle within twentieth-century humanism, that continues to this day: is humanism a substitute religion, and can science provide everything that religion once did, not least a basis for morality?

Bertrand Russell is a key player here, and we'll look at what he believed. Humanism in the twentieth century has also been close to many of the rights and freedoms that we all now take for granted.

Finally, we'll look at Christian humanism and the way various theologians have found that their faith traditions offer rich resources for looking at the world through human eyes and understanding the human condition.

Our examination of modern humanism, or rather humanisms, has now revealed not only advocates of the themes that reach back through the Enlightenment and to the Renaissance, but also critics of them, too. What is humanism? It is a human-centred concern with science, reason, personhood, happiness and freedom – and it is nothing if not richly diverse.

But there is perhaps one figure that the astute reader will have noticed has been missing until now. Moreover, he is particularly important since he plays a key role in debates about humanism that not only took place during the twentieth century but are alive and kicking in the twenty-first, right up to the present day. That figure is Charles Darwin (1809–82).

The Darwinian revolution

In the history of humanism, there are few commemorative dates. The year Pico published *On the Dignity of Man*, 1486, might be one; the day David Hume died, Sunday, 25 August 1776, might be another. But there is one more to add: 24 November 1859. On this day Darwin's *On the Origin of Species by Means of Natural Selection*, or the *Preservation of Favoured Races in the Struggle for Life* – the *Origin of Species* for short – was published.

His book is the foundational text for the scientific theory of evolution. Its key idea is that in nature, advantageous physiological variations are preserved according to whether an organism survives and whether it mates. This is called natural selection and sexual selection respectively. In fact, Darwin was not the first to propose a theory of evolution; that accolade goes to the pre-Socratic philosopher Empedocles of the fifth century BCE. However, the book is a landmark in modern humanism on a number of counts:

1 **Science** Darwin's big idea, evolution, is one of the most important theories in modern science. Its essence is that natural processes can account for the extraordinary

diversity of living creatures on earth through adaptive selection. Darwin had amassed very substantial evidence in support of his theory, evidence that has only increased as evolution has developed since.

2 **Religion** If evolution provides an explanation for the complexity of the living world, it also provides a rebuttal to proofs of God's existence by design. Although many philosophers, including individuals like David Hume, had suggested reasons as to why design might be doubted, the lack of an alternative explanation for the intricacy of the living world was a weakness in their critique. After all, the variety and mutual dependency of living organisms is extraordinary. Darwin allows atheists to propose why without resorting to God.

3 **Controversy** The book has been followed by wave after wave of controversy from the moment it was published. The arguments it sparks fall into two categories. First, the theory is probed on scientific grounds. For example, many scientists wondered what the mechanism for passing on changes across the generations might be. Darwin called his own theory of inheritance 'pangenesis' and it was roundly criticized by his contemporaries. The real answer emerged in two stages. First, genes were discovered in 1865, by Gregor Mendel and, second, the role played by DNA in genetic inheritance was revealed in 1943. That was an important gap in the theory filled – though other details of evolution continue to generate substantial and often fierce debate among biologists. Having said that, it should also be noted that none of them doubts the basic insights of evolution. That no mainstream biologist doubts the fundamentals of evolution is important to underline because the second category of controversy – on religious and moral grounds – can involve the denial of evolution. Darwin's theory is quite as earth-shattering as the Copernican revolution of the sixteenth century and the revolutions in relativity and quantum physics of the

twentieth. It took centuries for some to accept that the earth was not the centre of the universe. Arguably the philosophical implications of the work of Albert Einstein and quantum physicists like Niels Bohr and Werner Heisenberg are still hardly understood. So perhaps it is enough that the work of today is to come to terms with what Darwinism means for human beings.

The religious and moral controversies about evolution took shape very quickly and have remained pretty constant over the years. The questions that the debates revolve around include:

* What does evolution mean for the status of human beings alongside other animals?
* If it undermines any designing role for God in the universe, does it also undermine any human sense of meaning in the world?
* Since natural selection is purposeless, does that mean that all human life is purposeless too?
* If the dominant law among natural organisms is 'survival of the fittest' then does that release human beings from all moral constraints?
* If nature selects those creatures that are best adapted to their environment, then maybe human beings should follow suit and select people that they regard as superior too – the science of eugenics?

The Scopes trial

These controversies came to a head in the first decades of the twentieth century when they clashed, sometimes violently, with a new phenomenon: Christian fundamentalism. The word fundamentalism comes from a series of pamphlets called *The Fundamentals* that were published by American evangelicals during the 1910s and insisted on Christians believing certain things like the inerrancy of the Bible. Evolution came to be pitted against one of the tenets of such fundamentalist belief, namely creationism. Ironically, few people in Darwin's day – a generation or two before – believed in biblical literalism and whether or not, say, the Garden of Eden actually existed. It was not until the mid-1920s, most strikingly at the John Scopes 'monkey trial' in Dayton, Tennessee, that lines were drawn between this new strain of Christianity and the new science.

The trial concerned the prosecution of a science teacher for teaching evolution in a state school, which for a short while was illegal. Clarence Darrow, the agnostic defence lawyer, won the day. He humiliated the leading anti-Darwinian, William Jennings Bryan – though some commentators rather lament that Bryan was made to look so foolish. They suggest that thereafter the trial only served to entrench positions.

Having thrown all these questions up in the air, it is no surprise that Darwin supposedly called himself the 'devil's chaplain'. He has certainly become little short of a secular saint for many humanists, celebrated for the painstaking scientific work that blossomed into his theory and for the intellectual courage that could face its profound ramifications. Here, though, let us focus on two questions. First, what is the philosophical status of evolution as a scientific theory? This is important given that evolution is such a prominent bone of contention in the debates humanists have with their opponents in the modern world. Second, what exactly is the impact that evolution has on the philosophy of religion and the question of the existence of God?

Creationism and intelligent design

Understanding evolution's status as a scientific theory has become so important because of the battle pitched against evolution by creationists, alongside the proponents of a variant on creationism, so-called intelligent design. Though both have changed in the last century or so, the difference between creationism and intelligent design is roughly as follows:

* Creationists believe that the world was created in six days, as a literal reading of the book of Genesis in the Bible appears to imply.

* Intelligent design does not hold to that, but rather believes that there are gaps in the scientific account of evolution which can only be explained by God's agency. For example, they argue that science itself has thrown up examples from the anatomy of certain creatures that are simply too complex to have evolved by natural selection. In this way, intelligent design presents itself as scientific.

Mainstream science responds to these challenges in two ways:

* First, by demonstrating that all the examples the advocates of intelligent design provide in support of their theory are mistaken. Evolution can in principle explain them all.
* Second, by stating that God is not a scientific explanation of the natural world, being scientifically inexplicable himself. In short, intelligent design is not science. (Incidentally, mainstream biblical scholars provide the best response to the creationist's literalism by pointing out that there are actually two creation myths in the book of Genesis, and so to take either literally is in fact unbiblical.)

The politics of evolution

However, if that is how reason can dismiss the challenge of creationism and intelligent design, rhetoric often steals the show – and spreads confusion. For example, there is a tendency among some Darwinists to debate as if evolution was simply and indisputably true in all its parts. This strategy, I believe, actually prolongs the controversy.

Hence the need for a proper appreciation of evolution. It is vital to see beyond the crude blacks and whites of this increasingly politicized debate. And in order to do so, I offer just one philosophical consideration of Darwin's theory, that of the philosopher Karl Popper (1902–94).

Evolution as a theory

Popper was a leading philosopher of the twentieth century and is remembered for the way he thought science proceeded, as articulated in his book *The Logic of Scientific Discovery* (1934). According to him, scientists come up with theories based upon their intuition. These are then tested empirically. However, it is never possible to totally verify these theories – any more than it is possible to say for certain that the sun will rise tomorrow solely on the basis of the observation that it has risen for countless, previous yesterdays. Rather, Popper thought, the best scientific theories last because they are not shown to be false. To put it another way, the best scientific theories are those that would be the most easy to falsify. That they stand up makes them all the more likely.

Popper examined the theory of evolution for the parts that are, on his account, scientifically robust and for others that are based more on conjecture and/or are difficult to test. According to him, the indisputable aspects of evolution are those that concern adaptation. After all, it is almost tautologous to say that the offspring of an organism which, through random variations, turn out to be better adapted to their environment are bound to survive better. This is not to belittle evolution but to emphasize its power. What Darwin added – and this is his greatest scientific achievement, according to Popper – was showing that the evolution of a species will take place over very long periods of time.

Just how long, and whether perhaps there are periods in which evolution speeds up, or even appears to make jumps, is one of the contentious areas of modern evolutionary research. However, the basic timeframe is enormous – and note, quite long enough to throw the creationist's beliefs into disarray.

Alongside such strengths, Popper also raised several weaknesses. Take just one, the origins of life. Darwin himself did not discuss this matter in his book. It was as theologically a sensitive issue then as now, but more importantly in terms of science, natural selection presupposes that life exists already for it to work (hence the title *Origin of Species*, not *Origin of Life*). So strictly speaking, evolution can have nothing to say about the origins of life.

Having said that, a working theory that many biologists do try to test is that life arose spontaneously from some kind of primordial soup, perhaps in the forging of complex, organic molecules as a result of electro-magnetic reactions in the ancient terrestrial atmosphere. This notion is supported by Darwin in that he famously used the image of the tree of life to picture how species diversify. It suggests a common ancestry for life, hence the primordial soup theory. Popper thought this image leads to poor science since it is impossible to falsify. Conversely, it could be the case that life spontaneously emerged several times on planet earth. We just don't know and, at the moment, it looks like we probably never will.

Incidentally, there are other moments from within the history of evolution that are not easily accounted for by Darwin's theory. One is the appearance of eukaryotic cells, that is cells with nuclei and other features. These cells are those that make up nearly all multi-cellular organisms like animals and plants, including ourselves. The problem here is that their emergence seems fantastically unlikely, though obviously it has happened.

The emergence of consciousness seems to be another highly improbable event, though clearly it, too, exists. It will not be until science has a far clearer idea of what consciousness is that just what is at stake in this will itself become clearer. Though again, it is possible that science will never understand consciousness at all, as is believed by some philosophers.

Language

Other philosophers as well as Popper have highlighted problems with evolution. A striking one is the origins of language. Language is based upon rules and conventions. It is fundamentally different from the grunts and calls of non-human animals, so it cannot exist apart from the prior existence of a community of people who already share those rules and conventions. In other words, it seems that there can never have been an isolated individual who used language.

Natural selection, though, occurs as a result of variations embodied in isolated individuals. In order to have an evolutionary explanation for the origins of language, you would need to imagine an isolated individual first speaking. Again, this appears to be something of an impossibility.

Incidentally, there is evidence that some animals, like apes, can be taught some rudiments of language. They then communicate by, say, touching pictures. But that makes the same point: language must be taught; it has not arisen spontaneously, at least in these cases. This is to say that it already exists – in the communal capacities of the animals' human keepers.

Darwinism and purpose

So much for the achievements and gaps in evolutionary theory. What of its philosophical implications for religious belief? These can be broken down into two parts. First, on its implications for the purposefulness of life; and second, on its implications for the design argument and the existence of God.

The sense in which Darwinism can be taken to challenge the sense of life having a purpose concerns what is called teleology. Teleology is the idea that organisms and activities have a goal or end. Such final causes would drive an organism or activity forward. The search for them had been a tenet of the explanation of things since the time of Aristotle, who first systematized teleology in his metaphysics. Moreover, Aristotle talked about such goals and ends as good for the organism or activity concerned.

Darwin undermines this purposefulness because evolution by natural selection has no final goal. It happens randomly in the now with no thought for the morrow. Evolution cannot even be said to have the goal of survival: rather it is that those creatures which happen to survive that pass their characteristics on. So, the proto-spider developed the capability of spinning webs not because that would then enable it to catch flies – as if that goal was always pulling the evolution of the spider in that direction. Rather, the proto-spider gradually developed the capability of spinning silk which as it turned out is good for catching flies. Thus, put crudely, the best spinners of webs survived.

It should be noted that it is easy to forget that evolution is purposeless. The move from saying simply that such and such a feature evolved, to saying it was adaptively advantageous, to saying it evolved because of the advantages it conferred on the organism is a small one, especially when such features seem truly extraordinary viewed with hindsight. And yet that move reintroduces a false sense of teleology into the equation. It seems a hard belief to put down.

Values

There is another factor to remember here. Even if it is acknowledged that Darwinism renders natural life purposeless, there is a long tradition in philosophy of recognizing that values cannot be found in the natural world anyway – the so-called naturalistic fallacy. David Hume summed it up by saying that people often make an unwarranted assumption that an 'is' implies an 'ought'. That might lead to the conclusion that we are our own source of values. It is not that an exquisitely beautiful flower or wonderfully made insect in themselves has meaning, it is that we see meaning in the exquisitely beautiful flower and wonderfully made insect. As Bertrand Russell put it, when it comes to values, 'We are kings and we debase ourselves if we bow down to nature.'

Evolutionary ethics

This raises another aspect of evolutionary theory – one that aims precisely to answer this question – namely evolutionary ethics, the attempt to understand morality from within an evolutionary frame. The driving idea is that given human beings evolved, then their moral sensibilities must have evolved too – in the Darwinian sense. Thus, it should be possible to understand ethics in evolutionary terms.

In general, this is taken to mean that things are afforded ethical value in accordance with their adaptive advantage. For example, human beings assign friendship a high moral worth because friendly behaviour among evolving human beings was beneficial to their survival. Similarly, altruism is widely regarded as a good trait but only because considering others served the self-interests of individual members of the human species at some time in the past. However, there are substantial scientific and philosophical problems with evolutionary ethics:

1. **History** Explanations of moral behaviour tend to presume specific knowledge of the social life and conditions of human beings in the Pleistocene period in which they are said to have evolved. However, scientific knowledge of this period at this level is very sketchy. So, as a general rule, the conclusions that evolutionary ethics draws when assuming knowledge of this period is highly speculative and almost wholly untestable.
2. **Reductionism** A related criticism is that evolutionary ethics often crassly reduces complex human feelings and decisions to fit it into the Darwinian frame. Considering friendship again, friendship is taken to be defined as something like mutual goodwill resulting from mutual benefits exchanged – that is, as something essentially instrumental. The philosophers of friendship, though, all agree that the best kind of friendship is not instrumental at all. In fact, if it is perceived primarily as such then it is undermined – as in someone feeling that they are 'being used'.
3. **Purpose** Another problem with evolutionary ethics is that evolution itself is neither good nor bad; it is purposeless. So to ascribe ethical feelings to evolutionary processes is mistaken because it introduces meaning into the system.

To put it another way, it is an occasion of the naturalist fallacy, the mistake of deriving a value from a fact. For example, the society of humankind is a biological fact, but its moral significance – given that it is taken to have moral significance – has other origins, in sentiment or politics.

4 **Determinism** From these critiques come others that might be even more concerning for humanists. For example, evolutionary ethics is deterministic. It sees human beings as biological animals that are controlled by their genes and the environment. This means that human beings are merely 'survival machines', robots without any real subjectivity. The self is an illusion; autonomy is no more than self-control. We are predestined, as it were, to act in certain ways – an understanding of human nature that bears a striking resemblance to the predestination theologies of the Reformation, when human free will was similarly denied.

Complexity as a goal?

A second area in which teleology is vigorously debated concerns a different science, that of cosmology. The question here is whether the universe itself is goal-directed – whether by mechanistic means, it works towards the end of producing living creatures – and living creatures with self-awareness too.

Some biologists believe that there is a tendency in evolution to produce ever-more complex organisms that then find their greatest expression in the evolution of consciousness. Others deny that possibility, arguing instead that consciousness is an evolutionary exception but no more significant than, say, the marsupial's pouch or a giraffe's long neck.

The possibility that the universe itself might have goals is kept alive by the work of cosmologists. For example, they notice the fine tuning of many of the fundamental constants of nature. If these values had differed by even the tiniest fraction – fractions far too small to visualize – then the universe as we know it could not exist. This so-called anthropic principle, the idea that the universe appears tuned to allow humans to appear, can be refuted by pointing out that if the universe were not as it is, then we would not be here to observe it and imagine that an anthropic principle existed. Perhaps there are millions or trillions of universes, the refutation continues, where the constants are not as they are here, and there is no life to notice it. Proponents of the principle reply that speculation about the multiverse may or may not be right but, if it is, then it commits you to believing that there are not just trillions but zillions of universes 'elsewhere' – which seems at least as fantastical as any belief in teleology.

The debate continues.

Darwinism and God

When it comes to the design argument and the existence of God, Darwin's questioning presence is powerfully felt. Again, the controversy goes back to the earliest days. One infamous incident concerns Thomas Henry Huxley (1825–95), the Victorian anatomist and staunch defender of evolution. He approved of his sobriquet, 'Darwin's bulldog'. According to reports, in 1860, the year after publication, Bishop Samuel Wilberforce, son of the anti-slavery campaigner, had enquired of Huxley in a debate whether he was 'related to an ape on his grandfather's or grandmother's side?' Huxley's reply was equally withering. He said he would rather have an ape for a grandfather than a man who substituted ridicule for science. Incidentally, Huxley himself was an agnostic. Indeed, he invented the word to describe his position.

The argument for God's existence by design has been described as the one 'proof' that survived the Enlightenment onslaught against the other ontological and cosmological arguments. For example, even a sceptic like David Hume affords a respectful consideration of it in his *Dialogues Concerning Natural Religion*. However, with Darwin that final prop appears to collapse. The nub of the issue is usually taken to be that evolution undermines divine design, in the world of living organisms at least.

And yet, the situation is not quite so simple. For example, theists have argued that Darwin did believers a service in revealing the mechanisms by which God forged the living world. Darwinists reply that the most important element against design is the purposeless of evolution. Adaptation positively excludes the possibility of input from any intelligence. But the theist can reply: actually what Darwin's theory shows is that any *particular* adaptation is devoid of intelligence. The *ultimate* reason that adaptation occurs at all, though, can – if someone so wills – still be put down to a divine intelligence.

Again, the philosophical argument is far from resolved.

Organized humanism

Let us take a step back now and consider the story of humanism not as a philosophy but in its organized forms. Societies and organizations with explicitly humanist aims and goals began to take shape in the nineteenth century. An important date, and a good starting point for us, is 1851. For in this year, George Jacob Holyoake declared a 'secularist doctrine' from what he called the Central Secularist Society in London.

A note on secularism

The word 'secular' alone simply relates to worldly things. It marks the contrast with sacred things. It comes from the Latin for temporal. In politics, it identifies the separation of the state from the control of the Church – as in a 'secular state'. Secularization is the process by which this comes about. It is a settlement that the vast majority of people in the West – religious or otherwise – would subscribe to.

'Secularism' takes the meaning of the word a step further. It implies a rejection of religion, particularly in ethics. Having said that, a rational foundation for moral philosophy is something that many religious people would subscribe to as well – though they might add that religion provides a powerful motivation for behaving morally.

Here, then, I will use the phrase 'atheistic humanism', a phrase once used by the philosopher Antony Flew, to refer to those who explicitly reject any kind of religious worldview.

Holyoake's secularist doctrine featured elements such as that science and reason are the only authorities for empirical and moral knowledge; that morality should be guided by utilitarianism; and that the positive philosophy of Comte should be 'the scientific Bible of secularism'. Throughout the 1850s, Holyoake organized conferences and published newspapers and books promoting these causes. He garnered support from individuals and other societies with related aims, and campaigned on various issues from allowing park bands to play on Sundays to the repeal of the blasphemy laws.

Another key person emerged at the end of the decade, Charles Bradlaugh (1833–91). In his *Autobiography*, John Stuart Mill described Bradlaugh as 'a man of ability', who shared 'the democratic feelings of the working classes, judged political questions for [himself] and had courage to assert [his] individual convictions against popular opposition'.

Bradlaugh was instrumental in founding the National Secular Society in 1866 – a society that still thrives. As its first president, Bradlaugh championed the principles of promoting human happiness, and removing religious and legal barriers to free thought and life. And its establishment was hard fought. The humanists were involved in public events, some controversial and stormy, and campaigned on various social issues including birth control, poverty, religious education and religious broadcasting. Being involved could be dangerous. On occasion humanists were imprisoned. One individual, Annie Besant, had custody of her child removed on account of her views.

Perhaps unsurprisingly, given what was at stake, individual humanists often disagreed on questions of strategy and ideology. Should they campaign directly against religious beliefs or just the hold that religious policies have on society? Should they adopt Comte's positivism as Holyoake believed, or some other version of humanism? Bradlaugh argued for attacks on theology and was against Comte's positivism (which was labelled 'Roman Catholicism minus the Christianity'). He won the day.

Publications

By 1885, Charles Watts had begun publishing *Watts' Literary Guide*, a publication that was revised, and lives on now as the magazine, *New Humanist*. Watts also organized the Propagandist Press Committee that is now part of the Rationalist Press Association. The *Thinkers' Library* was another landmark in the history of modern humanism. It published 140 volumes over 22 years, including works by Mark Twain and H. G. Wells.

Across the first years of the twentieth century, the National Secular Society reached new peaks in terms of membership and attendance at the public events it sponsored. It had entered the mainstream. And then, a particularly notable event occurred. In 1927 the celebrity British philosopher Bertrand Russell lectured the society on the theme of 'Why I am not a Christian'. The lecture was subsequently published and, ever since, Russell has been held in high regard by humanists, atheist and otherwise.

Russell the man

Russell liked to keep people guessing about his personal convictions. While he popularized many arguments against organized religion and theistic belief, he described himself not as an atheist but as an 'atheistically-inclined agnostic': there is always room to doubt the non-existence of God, he teased. Similarly, while he became closely linked to the secularist movements, he once told a journalist that he felt uncomfortable with humanism since 'I think, on the whole, that the non-human part of the cosmos is much more interesting and satisfactory than the human part.'

This wit is exhibited throughout Russell's essays on religion, too. In one he notes how bizarre it is that although the biblical injunction about keeping the Sabbath is to do no *work* on a Saturday, certain Protestants reinterpret this to mean do not *play* on a Sunday.

Russell's objection to Christianity is robust and rests on two pillars of scepticism. First, he argues that to be a Christian requires belief in God and immortality. Second, he argues that it necessitates holding, 'that Christ was the best and wisest of men'.

1 Proofs fail

Russell does not believe in God for the reason that the traditional proofs of God do not persuade him. He is not alone in this: they have not persuaded many others, before and since. Nevertheless, as it happens, some of Russell's reasons for not believing the proofs have fallen out of date. Consider the 'first cause argument' – that God was needed to kick the world off. Russell followed the astronomers of his day who suggested that 'there is no reason to suppose that the world had a beginning at all'. However, astronomers do now say that the universe had a beginning – though whether or not it needs a 'first cause' to prompt it into existence is currently a moot point.

When it comes to immortality, Russell had addressed the issue in an earlier essay, *What I Believe*. He found against it on the grounds that human life seems so intimately tied up with material existence that it is just inconceivable that life could continue after the body dies. He also felt the belief that humans have immaterial souls made little sense since if they are immaterial then they would not be limited to one place but would presumably extend throughout the whole of space. That human beings always experience themselves as being only in one location would appear to be evidence against the existence of souls.

Russell went on to consider various moral reasons for belief in God – from the need to have God in order to determine what is right and wrong, to God's role in establishing justice. He finds them all at fault, and explains his deeper concerns too.

For example:

What really moves people to believe in God is not any intellectual argument at all. Most people believe in God because they have been taught from early infancy to do it, and that is the main reason.

This objection to the teaching of religion to children, widely observed to be the most usual cause of religious belief, is one that reaches across twentieth-century atheistic humanism. As the Jesuit motto has it: 'Give me a child until he is seven and I will give you the man.'

2 Jesus the man

When it comes to whether Jesus is the best and wisest of men, Russell actually finds much to commend Jesus as a moral teacher. For example, he thinks 'Judge not lest ye be judged' is excellent advice, and he opines that a very good principle is: 'Give to him that asketh of thee and of him that would borrow of thee turn though him not away.'

However, for all that some of Jesus' ethical maxims are good, he finds his moral character abhorrent. For example, the idea that some people will be cast into outer darkness for all eternity goes against every humanist principle, even when thinking about the most evil of people. All in all, Russell thinks that Jesus' tone can be strikingly intolerant – and not becoming of a sage.

Fear – the root of all religion

Fear is objectionable not only because it makes people fearful but because it is the father of cruelty – fear of being cursed, of death, or eternal damnation. Thus, for Russell, religion is behind all inhibitions on moral progress, if moral progress is defined as promoting human happiness, for the reason that religion is behind some of humankind's deepest and most profound fears – and needlessly so.

It is something to do with this violent tone that Russell connects to another objection, namely that faith in Christ has made people in history distinctly wicked. He writes:

> ***The more intense has been the religion of any period, and the more profound their dogmatic belief, the greater has been the cruelty and the worse has been the state of affairs.***

Russell can be forgiven for not knowing about the excesses of the atheistic regimes of communism in Russia and China; he was writing in 1927. So, the philosophical refinement of Russell's point is that it is not the object of someone's faith that deepens their capacity for evil, but the irrevocable nature of their commitment to that faith which counts. Someone who utterly believes in the supreme truth of science can be as heartless as any believer – as history subsequently showed.

Similarly, when Russell rages against, say, the Church's objection to birth control – which contributed to the spread of deadly diseases – he is right to blame that evil on blind faith, but wrong to present it as if ignorant ethical dogmas are a peculiarly religious vice. Russell himself held what he regarded as an 'enlightened' educational philosophy, based upon allowing children to be free. However, going to the school where he started to propagate this philosophy all but destroyed his son John.

Of his time, and timeless

However, for all his flaws, there is no doubting the thrust of Russell's argument and the appeal that it has had to the humanists of his audience then and since. Russell ends with a typically purple passage that explains why he still inspires a following:

> ***We ought to stand up and look the world frankly in the face. We ought to make the best we can of the world, and if it is not so good as we wish, after all it will still be better than what these others have made of it in all these ages. A good world needs knowledge, kindliness, and courage; it does not need a regretful hankering after the past or a fettering of the free intelligence by the words uttered long ago by ignorant men. It needs a fearless outlook and a free intelligence. It needs hope for the future, not looking back all the time toward a past that is dead, which we trust will be far surpassed by the future that our intelligence can create.***

Scientific humanism

We have had a short interlude to consider the contribution of Bertrand Russell. Returning again to the story of organized humanism from where we left off: after Russell, another crucial figure in its development was the British biologist Julian Huxley (1887–1975), grandson of 'Darwin's Bulldog', T. H. Huxley.

A biologist, philosopher, author and educator, Huxley was the first director of UNESCO and the first President of the International Humanist and Ethical Union. These two sides of his work he saw as intimately connected, hoping that UNESCO would develop a 'scientific world humanism' that could underpin a 'single world culture'.

He picked upon the phase 'scientific humanism' as it had previously been favoured by many socialists. They argued that the broader 'free thought' movement needed to coalesce around left-wing aspirations that they felt were captured in the term. Huxley liked to think of scientific humanism as a new 'religion of life'. He argued that if the scientific element was that which attended to matters of reason and fact, the humanistic would inject a necessary concern with values, spirit and fellowship. Or, to put it another way, science needs to be made humane to counter the default mode of its cold, objectivistic gaze. In a book illuminatingly entitled *Religion without Revelation* he wrote:

> ***Man can and should begin constructing a new common outlook, a new habitation for his spirit, new from the foundations up, on the basis of a scientific humanism.***

Then in 1940 he published another book entitled *The Uniqueness of Man*. Here he explained what he meant further:

> ***Scientific humanism is a protest against supernaturalism: the human spirit, now in its individual, now in its corporate aspects, is the source of all values and the highest reality we know. It is a protest against one-sidedness and fixity: the human spirit has many sides and cannot be ruled by any single rule.***

This position, nonetheless, kept Huxley open to religious influences. In the 1960s he showed his debt to the mystical thinker Teilhard de Chardin, writing an introduction to de Chardin's seminal work *The Phenomenon of Man*. And when *Religion Without Revelation* appeared in its final 1967 edition, he called for a 'new and permanent natural religion', that incorporated evolutionary and 'transhumanistic' elements.

Religious humanism

Meanwhile, in 1933, things were happening on the other side of the Atlantic. The American Humanist Association published the first humanist manifesto, which talked of 'religious humanism'. It noted widespread changes in religious beliefs and called for a revision of traditional attitudes: 'the vital movement now is the direction of a candid and explicit humanism'.

By using the word religion it did not want to associate itself with theological doctrines but to adopt a word that had always been associated with 'the highest values of life'. A new religion would form its hopes and plans 'in the light of the scientific spirit and method'. The affirmation of life was its goal.

Forty years later – and after another brutal world war – the second humanist manifesto adopted a different tone. It noted that science can bring evil as well as good. It no longer saw itself as a religious humanism, but while denying supernaturalism and theism, it did not reject religion outright. Signed by hundreds of intellectuals, and including 17 longer points, it embraced several varieties of humanism – scientific, ethical, religious and Marxist – and other positions including atheism, agnosticism, rationalism and liberalism.

Movement, manifesto or creed?

To put it another way, at this stage, organized humanism was struggling to embrace a dizzying array of positions. This is perhaps why, after the war, in England there were moves to adopt a less inclusive stance. Events helped to catalyze a new focus. For example, a report from the Church of England blamed what it called 'humanism' for a decline in belief and morality. One humanist, Archibald Robertson, replied with a mini-creed that still sounds contemporary: 'Whatever in the modern world is good, whatever is creative, whatever is hopeful, has its roots in humanism ... The humanist position is alone rational and right.' Then, in 1955, the radio broadcasts of Margaret Knight, later published as *Morals Without Religion*, explicitly defined humanism as against religion.

For all that, though, ambivalence about the word persisted. The British novelist and essayist, E. M. Forster (1879–1970), for one, intervened by asking himself how he defined himself. Not atheist, he wrote in a letter to a magazine: too crude. Not agnostic: too feeble. Not liberal: 'impossible'. The word humanist encourages 'bored withdrawal', though he thought it the best option. 'It expresses more nearly what I feel about myself ... Humanism covers my main belief and my main disbelief.' To put it another way, Forster did not want to campaign for humanism, but rather celebrate it. He continued:

> ***Humanism could better be honoured by reciting a list of the things one has enjoyed or found interesting, of the people who have helped one, and of the people whom one has loved and tried to help.***

There were other humanists who did not agree with Forster – and they would not withdraw either. Harold Blackham (1903–2009) was one of them, and another key player in this story. He had been working on what he regarded as the principles of humanism that were necessary if it were to be a serious movement. His 1954 *Essentials of Humanism* concluded:

> ***Humanism, then, is not a set of opinions, still less a rejection of any set of opinions. It is a body of central convictions about reason and science, freedom and morality, ideas and values, which requires commitment, choice, and action, for it requires the creation of a personal life of one's own and***

of a world, a human civilization. Therefore humanism is a call to all men, a vision of what is to be achieved.

Deists allowed

We are now edging towards the present day. The anti-religious version of organized humanism seemed to gain the upper hand again, at least in Britain, when Barbara Smoker became President of the National Secular Society in 1971, a post she held until 1996. She had once called humanism a 'natural religion' based upon 'spiritual communion', but in her 1973 booklet *Humanism* she came out against any association with religion whatsoever.

Another prominent individual who seemed to be lending his weight in the same direction was the philosopher Antony Flew. For him, it was the phrase 'scientific humanism' that appealed again. It implied putting the welfare of human beings first: 'scientific primarily as regards matters of fact; humanist concerning questions of value'. Flew argued that from this a commitment to atheism followed, since religious ethics must put God's will first, whereas humanist ethics prioritize the needs of human beings. Then in 1993, Flew published a book entitled *Atheistic Humanism* based upon his *Prometheus Lectures* at the State University of New York given in 1991. In it he defended more atheist presuppositions, not least that as atheists human beings gain an 'inalienable prerogative of responsibility'.

But as if to show that the word could never quite be pinned down, in 2004 Flew declared himself no longer an atheist but a deist. Some confusion followed as to just what caused Flew to change his mind, although he has affirmed his new commitment on a number of subsequent occasions. It seems he has been impressed by new arguments from philosophers of religion on the existence of God, troubled by the problems that naturalism has in showing how non-living matter can turn into living organisms, and intrigued by questions about the big bang and fine tuning raised by cosmology.

Nicolas Walter, in his detailed history of the term, *Humanism: What's in the Word* (1997), concludes that while there is still debate in humanist circles as to the stance it should adopt, humanism is 'generally seen as definitely separate from and indeed hostile to religion'.

Since then, with the increased prominence of apparently religiously inspired terrorism, and also because creationism seems to be taught more and more in schools, particularly in America, atheistic humanism has redoubled its energies. The high watermark to date came with the publication of *The God Delusion* by evolutionary biologist Richard Dawkins (b. 1941) in 2006. Though ferociously critiqued by believers and atheists alike, it was a runaway bestseller and sold millions of copies worldwide.

A new humanism?

Now that we are up to the present day, I must switch into a more personal mode of reflection. On the one hand, it seems to me that some of the charges being hurled at religion are right on target. For example, it is troubling that in some parts of the world, notably America, creationism is taught alongside modern science as if there were a choice between the two. Also, religions often continue to sanction prejudice against women and homosexuals, which results in untold human unhappiness, to say nothing of violence and deaths.

On the other hand, some of what is written and said by atheistic humanists against religion is either ignorantly simplistic or wilfully prejudiced. It is the tone that the new atheists have adopted – the strategy of vilifying those they see as opponents – that is so telling. Here are some of the things that they say:

* Religious people, without distinction, are against freedom, learning and culture.
* Their faith in God is said by definition to be no more subtle than believing in fairies or pixies.

* They are indirectly blamed for the violence of the terrorists: it is argued that moderate beliefs provide a cover for extremists by placing matters held on faith above contradiction.

The sociologist of religion, Gordon Lynch, has written: 'The sheer ferocity of many of the atheist critiques of religion also suggests that we are not in the territory of reasoned debate, but witnessing the birth pangs of a new, anti-religious cultural identity.' Lynch adds that whether this comes about remains to be seen. Or, as E. M. Forster intimated, it is an open question as to whether humanism can ever be that kind of thing anyway.

There are also atheists who believe that the present wave of religious lampooning is unhelpful, even opposed to the spirit that led them to atheism. Julian Baggini, author of *Atheism: A Very Short Introduction*, writes:

> ***I think that my opposition to militant atheism is based on a commitment to the very values that I think inspire atheism: an open-minded commitment to the truth and rational enquiry ... Hostile opposition to the beliefs of others combined with a dogged conviction of the certainty of one's own beliefs is, I think, antithetical to such values.***

The point is not just an important personal reflection but carries political weight: in an era of religious fundamentalism and violent extremism, Christian and atheistic humanists should surely be working towards a common cause to combat growing intolerance.

Christian humanism

In fact, humanism inspired by Christianity – and humanists who are Christians – have been integral to the humanist tradition ever since the Renaissance. Moreover, in recent years Christian humanists have been putting every bit as much work into redefining themselves as their atheistic peers. They argue that many of the elements within religious belief that non-believers find so objectionable are ones that repel them too. So who are the key figures in Christian humanism and how do contemporary Christian humanists define themselves?

The problem of sin

There is a sense in which Christianity might be thought to be an almost naturally humanistic religion. Its central figure is a man, Jesus. Moreover, this human being is said to be divine. On the face of it this incarnation would seem to provide an excellent framework within which to place many of humanism's great themes – its celebration of the dignity of humankind, human solidarity, freedom and knowledge. These elements do capture the essence of the beliefs of Christian humanists.

However, not all traditions within Christianity have interpreted their faith in the God who became man as so effusive of humanity. For example, Calvinist theology does not recognize the innate dignity of human beings. It surveys all the evil that exists in the world and concludes that human nature is depraved by sin. Martin Luther similarly thought that free will is delusional since human beings are corrupted. That God had become man was to rescue humanity from this fatal predicament, not to endorse it. For these Protestant theologians, Jesus saves human beings, not sanctifies their humanity.

It is a question of degree. There is one tradition in Christianity, reaching back to the great theologian of the fourth century, Augustine, which views humanity as 'a mass of sin, waited upon by death', as Augustine uncompromisingly put it. Humankind's present state is a product of the Fall, the mythical original sin of Adam and Eve. It was catastrophic. However, there is another tradition in Christianity that is inspired by the words of God in Genesis. After having created the world and all that lives in it, the story goes that God looked and declared it was good.

Creation is good

The great theologian of the medieval period, Thomas Aquinas, was more inclined in this direction. For him, the great capacities of human beings – to love, to reason, to create – reflect the nature of God. Moreover, God sustains life every moment of the day. It is hard to have a completely negative view of something with which the all-good God is so actively involved, though Aquinas undoubtedly thought that God's needful grace was part of that activity if human beings are to be perfected again.

Christian humanists today might also believe that God's intervention, in some shape or form, is necessary for human beings to live fulfilled lives. Far from seeing this as a weakness, though, they argue that it is a serious response to a serious problem within humanism – the fact that humanity has such a tremendous capacity for evil.

Theological humanism

To flesh this out a little further, consider now some of the key figures in Christian humanism, starting first with Dietrich Bonhoeffer. Bonhoeffer (1906–45) was a German Lutheran theologian. During the rise of Nazism, he was a member of the Confessing Church that tried to oppose Fascism. In 1943, Bonhoeffer was arrested for his involvement in a plot to overthrow Hitler. This led to his imprisonment and execution in 1945, aged 39.

Bonhoeffer is distinctive because of his radical interpretation of the incarnation of God in the person of Jesus Christ. He eschewed speculative theology about God's otherworldliness, as well as highly spiritualized religious ideas of God within us. For him, God *was* the human being Jesus Christ. This person vicariously suffered for others and thereby showed humanity at its best to be 'being for others'. After Christ's death, Bonhoeffer believed Christ was resurrected in the Church. So, therefore, all Christians are called to live for their fellow humans.

This humanistic theology led to a polemic against religion. In fact, Bonhoeffer thought that organized religion was the product of sin. It inevitably makes God out to be either wholly transcendent or individualistically present in the believer. Both are misconstrued since they result from the selfish desires of men and women. In other words, his Christianity is explicitly non-religious and this-worldly; it is a secular Christianity – to the extent that some of his followers have interpreted him as meaning that Christians should live as if there is no God. Bonhoeffer also declared that the modern world has 'come of age', by which he meant that it could be accountable to itself. In this way we can be mature.

Bonhoeffer is an important figure for Christian humanists because of the example of his life. Other theologians are invoked because they are some of Christianity's biggest hitters. For example, in the early nineteenth century, Friedrich Schleiermacher (1768–1834) wrote explicitly against Christianity's opponents, or its 'cultured despisers' as he called them. He argued that every human being can have what he called 'God-consciousness'. The significance of the person of Jesus is that he perfected his God-consciousness naturally in his own life. This is what makes him so central for Christians. He is the example that all human beings may follow.

Schleiermacher was also against supernatural understandings of faith, writing: 'The idea that the divine revelation in Christ must be something in this respect supernatural will simply not stand the test.' For him, to be religious, is to have a 'sense and taste for the infinite'. Monotheism was simply the purest form of this feeling for the absolute.

Alternatively, the Catholic theologian Karl Rahner, a leading twentieth-century figure associated with the Second Vatican Council, echoes other humanist sentiments on the dignity of humankind:

> ***Only someone who forgets that the essence of man is to be unbounded ... can suppose***

that it is impossible for there to be a man, who, precisely by being man in the fullest sense ... is God's existence in the world.

(*Theological Investigations*)

Sea of Faith

Christian humanism took a distinctive turn in 1980 when a Cambridge academic and priest, Don Cupitt, published a book, *Taking Leave of God*. In it, Cupitt presented a history of Christianity that exemplified the so-called 'death of God' theologies. Taking Nietzsche's exploration of the emergence of the modern world seriously, he reinterpreted the incarnation again – this time to mean that the centre of religious concern has moved from God to humanity, from heaven to earth. This changes what Christians might think about God. Instead of being a supernatural entity, Cupitt wrote that God becomes 'a unifying symbol that eloquently personifies and represents to us everything that spirituality requires of us'. As a result, Christianity comes to celebrate selflessness in life and not belief in the objective reality of God or life after death.

Cupitt develops his form of Christian humanism in other ways. For example, he acknowledges that the veracity of Christian dogma rests on its moral authority as opposed to its objective truth. The objective truth of God – theological 'realism' – simply cannot be ascertained. Christianity matters only in its championing of humanist values. He writes:

We cannot in fact be realists, for we all of us treat a serious moral objection to a dogma as a weighty reason for doubting its truth. This in turn implies that our real view of religious truth must be ethical.

This non-realism or atheistic attitude towards any objective belief in God is the cornerstone of a network Cupitt has inspired called the 'Sea of Faith' (after Matthew Arnold's famous line and an eponymous television series Cupitt presented). It is important to note that not all Christians who regard themselves as humanists are atheistic. However, Cupitt represents a point at which atheistic and Christian humanism come remarkably close.

Summary

In this chapter we have reached the present day in the history of humanism, and have also come up squarely against the most vigorous current debate within humanism, namely whether or not humanism can in some sense be religious. By way of a conclusion to this chapter, here are some questions that strike me as important to ponder as you consider what you think about this issue:

Three questions for atheistic humanists

1. In your arguments against religion do you examine the best in religion? After all, you look to the best in humanity in your humanism and engage the most sophisticated sources when asking scientific and philosophical questions.
2. Is it really true, considering the whole humanist tradition, that humanism can be straightforwardly defined by its opposition to belief in a supernatural God?
3. Is atheistic humanism not just optimistic but utopian, dangerously deluded about the depths of human depravity that undeniably exists in the world?

Three questions for Christian humanists

1. How is it possible to justify following so closely one particular man, Jesus, a Jewish eschatological prophet who lived 2,000 years ago?
2. Can you really claim to be humanist when Christian churches, even liberal ones, still fall foul of central humanist causes such as rights for homosexuals and women?
3. How can Christianity respond to modern pluralism, in which sincere individuals hold differing conceptions of what it is to be human?

4

humanism as a way of life

Many great themes have recurred through this book, from the importance of critique and reason, through the challenges of science and history, to the relationship between religious belief and humanist anthropocentrism.

In this last chapter, let us ask ourselves where humanism is at now, how humanists are inspired by the tradition today, and what challenges it faces for tomorrow.

Humanism in crisis?

It is possible to tell the story of humanism roughly as follows. Around 500 years ago, the medieval worldview – with its seamless integration of social, political and religious life – started to unravel. With the advent of the Renaissance, people began to develop a different sense of their worth; they sensed a dignity that was theirs without the necessity of making reference to God. At the same time, the old enchanted world – in which spirits abounded and physical objects like relics carried magical powers – was demythologized by early science. The earth was no longer the centre of the universe, and mechanical explanations for things showed astonishing power and promise.

The Reformation sealed and amplified these shifts. The hierarchies that were the fabric of medieval religious society were levelled in the experimental cities of reformers like Luther and Calvin: now everyone could aspire to the kind of human flourishing that previously had been the preserve of aristocrats and clergy. The process of disenchantment continued as the reformers declared the old system of relics, sacraments and indulgences superstitious nonsense – or worse, explicitly of the devil. From the sixteenth century onwards the conditions were optimal for the new science to prosper, which it did, for all that its greatest figures like Newton were obsessed with alchemy too.

The end of faith?

Then in the eighteenth century came the Enlightenment, when reason got to work on superstition, individual autonomy developed firmer foundations, the Church sustained a broadside that in terms of secular power weakened it, and philosophers established the basic framework within which people could lead a secular life: they could claim to be moral without religion and to find meaning and happiness without God.

In the nineteenth century, thinkers came to assume that religion would eventually disappear; faith was apparently retreating like the ebbing sea. One explanation of this change was provided by philosophers like Marx. They saw religion as the product of feudal discontent among the masses. As people's lives improved, they would no longer need the opiate. Coupled to this, the arguments that undermine religion – the rational demolition of the proofs for God and so on – would gradually persuade more and more people. When Darwin announced his theory of evolution, progress finally seemed indisputable and inevitable to many. Society itself could now become rational.

A post-secular society

During the twentieth century things grew more complicated again. Two world wars shocked human beings out of any easy assumptions about their dignity; as Sigmund Freud commented, civilization is 'thin'. The totalitarianism of Stalin and Mao, and the development and use of nuclear weaponry, destroyed any automatic link between science and progress. And as the world became more globally connected, people came to feel more disconnected, with the result that, for many, religion seemed to provide increasingly attractive ways of belonging.

By the end of the century, an inevitable process of secularization was no longer plausible, let alone the conviction that today we can look forward to the end of faith. In America, Christianity is more powerful than it was when the Puritans first landed from Europe. In South America, South Asia, the Middle East and Africa, religions are in rude health. Even in secular parts of the world – like China or Western Europe – belief is resilient and arguably resurgent. Though the figures are hotly contested, the 2001 census showed that 72 per cent of Britons called themselves Christian, even though only ten per cent regularly went to church. If you factor in the rise of New Age beliefs, then it seems clear that the vast majority of people still think of themselves as spiritual or religious in some way or other.

The debate changed

However, this does not mean that humanism is in decline. In fact, there is plenty of evidence that more individuals feel themselves to be humanists too – in the sense that they look to science for their understanding of the universe, make ethical decisions without explicit reference to religious authorities, and regard concern for their fellow human beings as a primary consideration in politics. The number of humanists seems to be between 15 and 30 per cent of the population. To put it another way, humanism and religious sensibilities are not necessarily incompatible; the relationship between them is not always a zero sum game.

What has undoubtedly changed in the last 500 years is that people have a choice. In a way that was inconceivable in the centuries before the Renaissance, individuals now routinely rub up against some people for whom religion determines their sense of themselves, others for whom religion is entirely and happily absent, and others again – perhaps a majority – for whom belief is one factor among many that shapes their world. Similarly, science did not win the war against religion, if that metaphor of violent annihilation is the appropriate one to deploy, but it did fundamentally change the terms of debate.

So today, it is perfectly possible to hold that only a thorough-going materialist rationalism makes sense, even as others assert that the world never really lost its supernatural enchantment, and others again sense that a scientific outlook alone is not enough, and the lack must be made up by moral, aesthetic, political and/or spiritual points of view.

Secular strength

The notion of a secular society is strong in the West, too, in the sense of the separation of Church and state. Within the European Union it is inconceivable that this could be fundamentally undermined, for all that there are marginal concerns over issues like creationism and faith schools. In the US – where it is impossible to be president without declaring yourself a Christian – the constitution has nonetheless withstood the rise of the religious right without difficulty, notwithstanding important battles over certain human rights that require protecting or remain to be won, say, in relation to gay people.

What this all adds up to is not that humanism has failed because it has failed to rid the world of belief or at least forced religion into a wholly private and therefore hidden sphere. Such an exclusive humanism – humanism as an anti-religious worldview – was only ever one element within the full range of humanist opinion. What 500 years of human history have brought about is a taming of religious excesses on a scale that was common during the wars of religion; a widespread habit of respect for others of different positions and beliefs; the social and political institutions that enable people to coexist even when they radically disagree.

An uneasy pluralism

And yet, there is no room for complacency. The world never stands still and continual, universal progress towards a utopian tomorrow is, I believe, a delusion. Terrorism is a persistent threat. War, poverty and exploitation do not cease. Consumerism – as secularism has shaped up in the West – seems humanly unsatisfying, if indicators such as rates of depression and social fragmentation are correct. It is quite easy to imagine that climate change, coupled with other political and economic factors, will radically destabilize the world. The President of the Royal Society – that venerable institution, the inspiration of which is the Renaissance humanist Francis Bacon – is Professor Martin Rees. He has calculated that human beings stand only a 50:50 chance of surviving the twenty-first century.

So the challenge to contemporary humanists is to carry forward this uneasy pluralism into the future. The hope that all people would share the same religious or humanist outlook was always a pipe dream, though it is one some theists and atheists alike still maintain.

The search for meaning

So much for the political agenda that humanism faces. What of more personal issues and the question of meaning? In a world of coexisting and sometimes competing frames of understanding, the question of what gives life meaning can seem under threat for the very reason that there is, apparently, more than one answer. This can imply to some that meaning comes à la carte, which doesn't seem very meaningful, or that, inasmuch as the choices conflict, the modern quest for meaning is cursed by confusion.

Humanists have suggested that meaning comes in a variety of ways:

1 A scientific way of life

There is a scientific pursuit of meaning based on the following principles:

* Science and technology offer the best means of finding practical ways of increasing human well-being and therefore meaning – notably in terms of physical health but, as science progresses, in terms of psychological and even moral well-being too.
* Rational thought is able to sift the various questions that human beings have traditionally associated with meaning in order to discard those that make no sense, and promote those that are worthwhile. For example, life after death as a source of meaning can be discarded, not just because there is no such thing but because if life is not good now there is little sense in prolonging it indefinitely in eternity.
* Alternatively, the pursuit of happiness is a rational objective – be that found in sustainable pleasures or the love of life and others – since happiness is its own

justification. Science and reason can tell us much about how to optimize our chances of success in this respect.

2 A narrative way of life

Alternatively – though in truth, these alternatives are not necessarily mutually exclusive – there is the use of stories to provide a sense of direction; in short, a narrative sense of meaning in life:

* Science is not enough for meaning or well-being. This is because science is objective and meaning is a subjective matter; science is about facts and meaning is about value; science seeks knowledge whereas meaning requires wisdom.
* What stories provide is a store of narratives about particular people and times that address the subjective matters of value and wisdom. Within these narratives individuals can associate and situate their own experiences to understand and interpret them better. Similarly, non-narrative art – like much music or visual art – is valuable.
* Narratives are not absolute in the sense that they do not apply to, or work for, everyone equally. Having said that, they do often contain strikingly similar themes and aspirations that enable us, through them, to connect with others in a way that is also meaningful.

3 A humanitarian way of life

Another source of meaning that is arguably more demanding, but perhaps ultimately more rewarding, too, is found in humanitarian action – humanism as practical charity, it might be said:

* Modern science and technology shows us that suffering through illness and poverty is widespread throughout the world. However, it also provides us with the means of alleviating this distress.
* Implicit in the concept of humanism is a call to care for others since we are like them. Moreover, justice

demands it. This is meaningful activity because the suffering of another is alleviated, it is gratifying to have helped another, and because it suggests that for all the ills which exist in the world, good can prevail.

* A deeper sense of meaning comes about from helping others as well. It emerges from having empathy. Empathy takes us out of ourselves, and our personal petty worries, and enables us to see our lives in a wider context.

4 A religious way of life

Humanism does not necessarily exclude a religious sensibility. And there are grounds for a religious humanist's sense of meaning:

* Religious humanism recognizes that traditional conceptions of God often presented God as a kind of cosmic tyrant; similarly religion can appear to be a question of obeying rules; and religious authorities look morally oppressive.
* Instead, we need a more mature relationship to that which lies beyond us, that which can be called the divine. This is an attitude that does not seek absolute authority in moral matters but rather embraces the freedom to be responsible for yourself. Such responsibility is in fact a much better notion of what it is to live well. God comes to be seen as the wellspring for the richness of life itself, in all its fullness.
* Living a moral life is, therefore, to live life fully, to live life well, and to live life for others. Rather than trying to anchor a sense of meaning to some point outside of life, it finds meaning in saying an effusive 'Yes' to life, even in death. Religious practices, like prayer, church-going and 'good works', may often be couched in old language but, ultimately, are aimed at orienting lives towards the highest possibilities for human beings, envisaged in God.

5 A wonderful way of life

There may be more options to consider, but finally here, let me suggest the sense of meaning that arises from the sceptical strand within the humanist tradition. This is wonderful in the literal sense, in that it finds life engaging because it is full of wonder.

* The sceptical humanist accepts that human capacities and knowledge are finite. Moreover, he or she believes that many of the ills that destroy human well-being result from hubris – the denial of fallibility and limit. 'Man is quite insane,' wrote Montaigne. 'He wouldn't know how to create a maggot, and he creates gods by the dozen.'
* Life is therefore something of an art. Like a painting, that is confined to the frame and constrained by the paint, life is lived well according to what we make of the limited means at our disposal, namely ourselves, those with us, and the society in which we live.
* This is, therefore, an examined life. It is worth living when individuals strive to know themselves and cultivate a fascination with the world around them. Such contemplative wonder results in the effort simply to see – both that which is becoming better known and that which remains ultimately unknowable. Mortals only have their allotted span. But the wonder is that in it they can touch the mystery of existence itself.

An old question revisited

So what is humanism?

Humanism is not a specific doctrine or a unified system of thought. Rather it is a tradition that started in the Renaissance, gathered momentum during the Enlightenment, and became a key feature of the modern world. During this development it embraced a range of possible meanings, principles and practices. It is fundamentally an attitude or spirit that values learning, curiosity and imagination aimed at engaging with the questions of life – personal and political – that human beings face and indeed that make us human. There are therefore many flavours of humanism, many philosophers that can be used to underpin it.

Cosmic impiety and humility

The Renaissance is an inspiration, though not because it was a period in which human beings supposedly awoke from a dark age: the medieval period was one of extraordinary invention and accomplishment. Rather, it is because the Renaissance humanists were able to make something wonderful of their times – in their joy of discovery and the embrace of the new, their cultivation of character, political reform, critical questioning, passion and potential. This still speaks to us, half a millennium later.

Then came the Enlightenment. For David Hume, scepticism was the natural position for the Enlightenment thinker – scepticism about religion for sure, but scepticism about the fundamentals of science too. Hume was also sceptical about what he called enthusiasm, defined as 'presumption arising from success'. That could apply to triumphalist rationalism and scientism as much as religion.

Kant found Hume's scepticism profoundly unsettling. He wanted to put things on a firmer foundation. And he did so, but only by writing *Critiques*. In these *Critiques*, the key issue was understanding the limits of human knowledge. When Kant said that Enlightenment was maturity he meant being able to live with this finitude and not reach out for false certainty. So we have Enlightenment humanism as scepticism and grappling with the reality of human knowledge and experience.

I would actually relate this to a tradition within religion, though one that is lamentably in decline today, called the 'apophatic', meaning 'negative way'. It stands in marked contrast to the 'cataphatic', meaning 'positive way'; the strident assertions of indisputable religious dogma and divine truth.

The apophatic is a way of approaching what is ultimately unknown by identifying what that unknown cannot be. In religion it says God is not mortal (immortal), not visible (invisible) – note, saying nothing positive about God. Its spirit is captured in the biblical story of Moses climbing the mountain. As he went up and symbolically got nearer to God, he did not ascend into greater light and clarity, but deeper cloud and unknowing. Thus, at its core is a sense of the sacred – that which is far greater than you and so takes you out of yourself and into the unknown.

In a way, what the apophatic theologians explored was similar to what the sceptical Enlightenment philosophers like Hume and Kant articulated: both identify limits and seek intuitions of what lies beyond. It was called 'learned ignorance' by the first Renaissance humanist philosopher, Nicholas of Cusa, and he got the idea from Socrates. Socrates annoyed his fellow citizens in Ancient Athens because he showed that the key to wisdom is not how much you know but is understanding the limits of what you know. This dimension reaches back right to the antecedent origins of humanism. It runs right through any honest study of what it is to be human.

Today, humanism is at something of a crossroads, though not in the sense that it is about to disappear; far from it. Rather, humanism as a philosophy is contested. This is largely as a result of concerns about the rise of fundamentalist religion and related challenges to secularism. In response, there are atheistic humanists who want to make the definitive characteristic of humanism as being against religion, though to my mind they distort the humanist tradition and caricature religious belief in so doing. Also, they perhaps unconsciously distract themselves from questions that humanism itself must face, many of which have been implicit in the pages of our exploration here.

It would be better to admit that the debate about humanism is open. It is open for the very good reason that the question of how people might live is also open, at least in a free society. As Kant pointed out when asking what Enlightenment might be, it is nothing without vibrant debate in the public sphere, encouraging people into maturity.

It is also this dimension that to my mind is needed to combat contemporary fundamentalisms – religious and scientific

– particularly if you want to avoid becoming a humanist fundamentalist in response. It is a kind of committed agnosticism – a juxtaposition of words that only sounds strange, if it does, today.

Echoing the same spirit, the last word can come from a famous humanist and agnostic, though never quite atheist, Bertrand Russell. Towards the end of his *History of Western Philosophy*, he reflects on how human beings across the centuries have related to their potential and powers. Sometimes, he believes, they have been too humble. In other periods, too hubristic. And today? He worries that we are at risk of thinking of ourselves as gods.

> ***In all this I feel a grave danger, the danger of what might be called cosmic impiety. The concept of 'truth' as something dependent upon facts largely outside human control has been one of the ways in which philosophy hitherto has inculcated the necessary element of humility. When this check on pride is removed, a further step is taken on the road towards a certain kind of madness – the intoxication with power ... to which modern man, whether philosophers or not, are prone. I am persuaded that this intoxication is the greatest danger of our time, and that any philosophy which, however unintentionally, contributes to it is increasing the danger of vast social disaster.***

This 'cosmic impiety', the greatest danger of his time, shows no sign of passing. Humanists must ensure that they help mitigate it.